Cambridge Elements

Elements in Organization Theory
edited by
Nelson Phillips
UC Santa Barbara
Royston Greenwood
University of Alberta

ORGANIZATIONAL STIGMA

Bryant Ashley Hudson
IESEG School of Management

Karen D.W. Patterson
University of New Mexico

Lin Dong
University of Birmingham

Shaftesbury Road, Cambridge CB2 8EA, United Kingdom

One Liberty Plaza, 20th Floor, New York, NY 10006, USA

477 Williamstown Road, Port Melbourne, VIC 3207, Australia

314–321, 3rd Floor, Plot 3, Splendor Forum, Jasola District Centre, New Delhi – 110025, India

103 Penang Road, #05–06/07, Visioncrest Commercial, Singapore 238467

Cambridge University Press is part of Cambridge University Press & Assessment, a department of the University of Cambridge.

We share the University's mission to contribute to society through the pursuit of education, learning and research at the highest international levels of excellence.

www.cambridge.org
Information on this title: www.cambridge.org/9781009730525

DOI: 10.1017/9781009730853

© Bryant Ashley Hudson, Karen D.W. Patterson and Lin Dong 2025

This publication is in copyright. Subject to statutory exception and to the provisions of relevant collective licensing agreements, no reproduction of any part may take place without the written permission of Cambridge University Press & Assessment.

When citing this work, please include a reference to the DOI 10.1017/9781009730853

First published 2025

A catalogue record for this publication is available from the British Library

ISBN 978-1-009-73052-5 Hardback
ISBN 978-1-009-73051-8 Paperback
ISSN 2397-947X (online)
ISSN 2514-3859 (print)

Cambridge University Press & Assessment has no responsibility for the persistence or accuracy of URLs for external or third-party internet websites referred to in this publication and does not guarantee that any content on such websites is, or will remain, accurate or appropriate.

For EU product safety concerns, contact us at Calle de José Abascal, 56, 1°, 28003 Madrid, Spain, or email eugpsr@cambridge.org

Organizational Stigma

Elements in Organization Theory

DOI: 10.1017/9781009730853
First published online: October 2025

Bryant Ashley Hudson
IESEG School of Management

Karen D.W. Patterson
University of New Mexico

Lin Dong
University of Birmingham

Author for correspondence: Bryant Ashley Hudson, b.hudson@ieseg.fr

Abstract: The purpose of this Element is to provide a comprehensive overview of organizational stigma research development and to identify future research directions, focusing specifically on the organization as the level of analysis. It provides a historical and contemporary review of the organizational stigma literature, identifies the most essential topics of discussion when researching organizational stigma, and moves through them to highlight the most salient topics for future research. Organizational stigma is a multidimensional and multidirectional conception. While attached to the organization, organizational stigma is developed based on the evaluation of an attribute, characteristics, or behavior of the organization by an organizational audience. In other words, the stigma is in the eye of the beholder, a result of the socio-cognitive processes of heterogeneous audiences. The authors hope to illustrate the important role that stigma and other social evaluations play in organizations and their inherently inseparable role in society.

Keywords: organizational stigma, negative evaluations, social evaluations, stigma management, stigma review

© Bryant Ashley Hudson, Karen D.W. Patterson and Lin Dong 2025

ISBNs: 9781009730525 (HB), 9781009730518 (PB), 9781009730853 (OC)
ISSNs: 2397-947X (online), 2514-3859 (print)

Contents

1 Introduction   1

2 The Foundations of Organizational Stigma   5

3 The Development of Stigma Theory   14

4 Stigma in the Context of Other Social Evaluations   31

5 Future Research   36

6 Conclusion   46

   References   48

1 Introduction

1.1 Purpose and Background

In this Element, we offer a thorough review of the literature on organizational stigma. In recent years, social evaluations and their role in organizational and economic life have received increasing attention from strategy and organization scholars (Pollock et al., 2019). Organizational stigma is among one of the most studied social evaluations in management literature (Hudson & Okhuysen, 2009; Piazza & Augustine, 2022; Roulet, 2015; Vergne, 2012). It is defined as "a collective stakeholder group-specific perception that an organization possesses a fundamental, deep-seated flaw that deindividuates and discredits the organization" (Devers et al., 2009: 157). These flaws may be associated with the organization's behaviors, such as corporate malfeasance or bankruptcy (Sutton & Callahan, 1987), the customers that an organization serves (Hudson & Okhuysen, 2009; Tracey & Phillips, 2016), or the inherent features and association of the industry in which the organization operates (Piazza & Perretti, 2015; Vergne, 2012), such as the arms industry, which is associated with weapons and death (Vergne, 2012), and the sex industry (Ruebottom & Toubiana, 2021). Organizational stigma is thus a particularly rich field of study. While all social evaluations are powerful, stigma, once assigned by relevant audiences, is particularly difficult to lose. It has been associated with important organizational outcomes such as media attacks and scrutiny (Hampel & Tracey, 2017), losing support from inside and outside stakeholders (Tracey & Phillips, 2016; Vergne, 2012; Wang, Raynard, & Greenwood, 2021), and formal sanctions such as legal sanction and closure (Hudson & Okhuysen, 2009; Sutton & Callahan, 1987). Moreover, due to its focus on organizations and organizing processes that are deeply discredited by audiences, organizational stigma encourages us to recognize and comprehend phenomena related to organizations and organizing that might otherwise be overlooked or avoided, such as men's bathhouses and the sex industry (Hudson & Okhuysen, 2009; Toubiana & Ruebottom, 2022).

The purpose of this Element is to provide a comprehensive overview of organizational stigma research development and to identify future research directions, focusing specifically on the organization as the level of analysis. We intend to focus on the most essential topics of discussion when researching organizational stigma, and move through them to identifying the most salient topics for future research. To encompass the relevant literature, we take a broad view of organizations. Organizational stigma can refer to a single organization, a group of similar organizations stigmatized due to similar activities, or an entire industry category or organizational field. Moreover, organizational stigma is a multidimensional and multidirectional conception. While attached to the organization, organizational stigma is developed based on the evaluation of an attribute, characteristics, or behavior of the organization by an organizational audience. In other words, the stigma is in the eye of the beholder, a result of the socio-cognitive processes of heterogeneous audiences. Furthermore, although the stigma may be a widely held perception, it is not always universal as it is intertwined with the normative expectations defined by heterogeneous audiences comprising various groups of stakeholders.[1] Given the complexity of the subject matter, we continue by identifying why it is important to study organizational stigma.

1.2 Why Study Stigma

The study of organizational stigma is important for several reasons, including, as stated previously, that it is a fact of organizational life. If all organizations experience stigmatizing activities by some people at some time (Hudson, 2008), then if organization scholars are to understand organizations, they need to understand organizational stigma.

To be specific, first, stigma typically has very real and negative effects on both the organization itself and on the people who participate in that organization. Organizations with stigma often suffer from a lack of resources and network affiliations (Lashley & Pollock, 2020), withheld due to both the negative evaluations of the organization and the fear of moral taint, or transferred stigma, that is often an outcome of affiliation with such organizations. Also, stigma results from a shared collective perception among a critical mass of stakeholders that is associated with negative attributes. Organizations and their stakeholders may internalize these negative attributes associated with the organization, identifying with and embracing certain aspects (Helms & Patterson, 2014); experiencing shame, distance and loss (Creed, DeJordy, & Lok, 2010; Creed et al., 2014); or constructing defensive tactics, both within the organization and among external stakeholders (Ashforth & Kreiner, 1999; Ashforth et al., 2007). The insights that result from these types of situations allow researchers to better understand the significant consequences caused by organizational stigma, as well as the power that is eroded in or afforded to both stigmatized organizations and stigmatizing audiences.

Second, the study of organizational stigma not only increases understanding of the potential for harm among organizational participants but also elucidates how

---

[1] We take the view that, as stigma is a social evaluation held by audiences doing the evaluating, stakeholders are a subset of audiences. In other words, all stakeholders are audiences, but not all audiences are stakeholders.

firms and those associated with them can avoid or ameliorate that harm. This provides insight into how and why organizations use impression management, identity reinforcing activities, decoupling, and other organizational processes. For example, Hudson and Okhuysen (2009) found that men's bathhouses use a variety of boundary management techniques that serve to manage stigma transfer. These techniques are also used by less-stigmatized organizations, but are less apparent in more traditional settings. Impression management techniques may ward off or ameliorate stigma. One of the most influential studies on impression management by stigmatized organizations is by Elsbach and Sutton (1992). They examined the ways in which social action organizations that engaged in discreditable activities used the attention afforded by such activities to rally support for and awareness of their causes. Carberry and King (2012) also contributed to impression management research by studying corporations that were targets or potential targets of corporate deviance claims after the Enron scandal of 2001. They found that adopted practices that could demonstrate an organization's commitment to normative standards could be used to manage stakeholders' perceptions of the organization and its behaviors. In this case, organizations that might be targeted sought to provide substantive evidence regarding the internal adoption of credible business practices that were seen as counter to the fraud and corruption exhibited by Enron (Carberry & King, 2012: 1147). The adoption of certain practices as an impression management tactic is an important organizational process and such processes are often easier to spot and examine in stigmatized industries and organizations.

In essence, some stigmatized organizations provide settings that serve as extreme cases that, in turn, allow for the examination and understanding of a myriad of organizational processes (Harding, Fox, & Mehta, 2002; Hudson, 2008; Hudson & Okhuysen, 2014). These cases allow us to understand some of the underlying assumptions, beliefs, and norms that are expected but not necessarily communicated within organizational contexts. These are translated across settings and types of stigma and can be experienced by organizations that are not normally in a stigmatized category.

Third, the study of organizational stigma also provides a unique lens to capture the dynamics that other theories cannot (Hudson & Okhuysen, 2014; Hudson, Okhuysen, & Creed, 2015). For example, organizations carrying stigma or facing stigmatization provide contemporaneous settings of organizations at the boundary of multiple contesting or contradictory sets of institutions (Hudson, 2008), some of which may support and some of which may stigmatize focal organizations. Most empirical examinations of institutional contestation use a retrospective lens, examining that contestation after the "winner" within the conflicted scenario has been determined. This introduces the potential for survivor or winner bias, explaining why a certain outcome came to be, which may obscure the patterns or elements of luck or failed strategies that are often erased after the dust settles. By examining stigmatized organizations, the processes of contestation and of organizational responses to that contestation can be observed as they occur (Hudson & Okhuysen, 2014), although often in a much shorter time frame (due to the nature of the research and publication process). The study of stigmatized organizations also allows scholars of organizations to examine the dynamics of multiple stakeholder groups and social audiences, which can be seen in high relief in this context due to the contestation and contradictions between them, and those dynamics are consequential for all organizations.

Fourth, studying stigmatized organizations reveals the use of power and power dynamics in organizational life. Stigma is a form of social control. To stigmatize is to label, withhold resources, restrict affiliations, and ostracize. Studying both the nature of organizational stigma and those organizations that are stigmatized highlights and illuminates such exercises of power as they are manifested in society and organizations. The assignment, management, internalization, negation, and/or utilization of stigma all illuminate significant power differentials among a diverse set of organizational stakeholders, multiple social audiences, and contested institutional arrangements. The use of power and power struggles, including resistance and adaptations, exhibited in various value assignments and responses is significant for understanding how organizational actors make decisions and take action around a variety of organizational variables and strategies. These power differentials also have implications for the ways in which societal values and expectations change over time, including the ways in which other types of social evaluations are internalized by such a variety of social actors.

Last but not least, the study of organizational stigma is important as it allows us to use an inclusive approach to studying organizations by identifying and understanding often neglected or overlooked phenomena. Research on stigmatized organizations helps to highlight and study marginalized, disenfranchised, or alternative communities that are often overlooked in traditional organizational scholarship. For example, Wang and Tracey (2024) theorized how anti-stigma social movement organizations can leverage social media affordances such as visibility to reduce group stigma of members of the LGBTQ+ community. However, most studies on organizations tend to focus on those that enjoy broad-based social approval and are therefore large and significant social actors. This focus privileges those organizations and the communities that support them, obscuring smaller, less powerful communities and the organizations that serve them. As organization scholars, it is our responsibility to understand organizations and organizational life in its entirety, including alternative forms of organizing and the role of such organizations in society. Neglecting to do so perpetuates the marginalization of these communities and is not consistent with the principles of social justice and equity.

1.3 Process and Organization

In order to provide a through account of organizational stigma research, this Element proceeds as follows. We begin by discussing the history of stigma research focusing on several different areas of study. While we differentiate between organizational stigma and individual-level stigma, we acknowledge that the foundations of organizational stigma lie in the social-psychological level of analysis. We provide information and insights into this history and how it has shaped research on organizational stigma. Drawing from a diverse range of perspectives, including those of social psychologists, sociologists, anthropologists, communications scholars, healthcare researchers, and others with an interest in stigma, allows us to trace the theoretical roots of the development of the theory of organizational stigma. Second, we organize the research on the topic of organizational stigma based on the plethora of existing studies. This includes a comprehensive exploration of key concepts related to stigma, such as stigmatization and stigma transfer, as well as critical discussions on the various contexts and research methods used to examine stigma-related phenomena. Third, we differentiate organizational stigma from other types of social evaluations of organizations, elucidate the relationship between them, and investigate how these concepts may interrelate, offering intriguing opportunities for further investigation. Finally, we discuss the future research directions of organizational stigma based on the current state of research, emphasizing the need for additional inquiry to fill gaps in our knowledge of this complex social evaluation.

2 The Foundations of Organizational Stigma

2.1 Linking Individual and Organizational Influences

Organizational stigma studies have been conceptually informed by research into stigmatization and coping mechanisms of individuals (Durkheim, 1895, 1897; Goffman, 1963). Issues related to stigma, such as deviance, scandal, morality, and punishment, have evolved throughout human history. Furthermore, stigma arises from the complexities of human interactions stemming from the moral basis for understanding and defining stigma. The basis for understanding stigma, then, lies in the relation of an individual to others, be it through some abstract "other" or a clearly defined set of rules that define what is "normal." These relationships are present in numerous settings, and stigma and the myriad related concepts have been explored across domains such as religion, literature, art, music, medicine, and the social sciences.

Although many concepts related to stigma have been debated throughout history, Emile Durkheim is recognized as one of the first modern social scientists to examine the concept of stigma in its contemporary sense, with implications for organizational research. Perhaps best known for his work defining efficient methods of organizing work, Durkheim's influential book, *The Division of Labour in Society* (1893), addressed how stigma emerged from the division of labor based on ability and how capitalism could reinforce the distinctions among classes. Durkheim was also interested in traditionally stigmatized topics such as crime (Durkheim, 1895) and suicide (Durkheim, 1897), as well as the underpinning morality that drove the definitions, understanding, and stigmatization of those issues. Durkheim's work is defined as a precursor to much stigma research, because it identified the social differences and resulting devaluation of various social classes, behaviors, and ethnic groups.

Despite significant interest in the concept of stigma in the late nineteenth century, Erving Goffman's work (1963) is the most widely influential work on stigma as a separate concept, particularly within management research. Goffman's canonical work delineates the sources of individual-level stigma as abominations of the body or physical stigma, character flaws or character stigma, and the stigma of group identity or tribal stigma. These "discreditable marks" can lead to the denigration of an individual's social identity by relevant audiences. This categorization – character stigma, physical stigma, and tribal stigma – led others to examine why some members of society are excluded from mainstream society or even groups that might otherwise welcome them (Douglas, 1966; Grattet, 2011; Kristeva & Herman, 2010; Tyler, 2018).

Goffman also distinguished between concealable and unconcealable stigma, or those types of discreditable marks that can be kept hidden, such as sexual orientation or substance abuse, and those that cannot be kept hidden, such as certain types of mental illness or physical abnormalities. Unconcealable stigma can have drastic and highly visible results. These range from practices such as the hunting of individuals with albinism for their body parts (Cruz-Inigo, Ladizinski, & Sethi, 2011) to denying promotions or employment to individuals with physical disabilities (Hernandez et al., 2008; Vickers, 2015). The consequences of disclosing and managing concealable stigma can also be accompanied by extremely negative consequences. Such negative consequences can lead employees that have concealable stigmas to manage their stigmas in highly varied ways (Jones & King, 2014). Significant research has been devoted to managing the psychological and emotional toll of individual stigma and the individual processes involved, including shame (Creed et al., 2014), guilt (Patock-Peckham, Canning, & Leeman, 2018), aggression (Kalichman, 2013; Tsai et al., 2013), depression, and other health and biological consequences (Chaudoir, Earnshaw, & Andel, 2013). This stream of research has played a significant role in examining the role of stigma in human resources concerns, such as discrimination, hiring preferences, and benefits (Dean, 2010, 2011; Hernandez et al., 2008; Timming et al., 2017; Vickers, 2015).

Another important contribution was Goffman's assessment of how the stigmatized manage their relationships with others who are not stigmatized. He differentiates between what he labeled the "own," the "wise," and the "normal." The "own" are those that recognize and internalize the stigma assigned to them. These stigmatized individuals often engage in various stigma management behaviors and may relate to others who are not stigmatized but are aware of the stigma and internalize it as part of their identity. By comparison, the "wise" are not stigmatized themselves but may be advocates for those that experience stigma. Advocating for the "own" is a role often associated with individuals or organizations associated with stigmatized populations. This may come in the form of support (Tracey & Phillips, 2016) or funding (Carberry & King, 2012). For example, although most Abrahamic religions do not support LGBTQ+ populations, certain denominations are categorized as GLAD (gay and lesbian affirming denominations) or Open and Affirming, meaning that they support LGBTQ+ members and permit openly LGBTQ+ candidates to be ordinated. These denominations may include many or no LGBTQ+ members but, through their support of the LGBTQ+ population in general, would be considered the "wise." The "wise" may experience stigmatization as a result of stigma transfer, which is also addressed in this manuscript (see Section 3.3.6). Finally, Goffman defines the "normal" as "non-deviants" who are in the position to label and discriminate against the "own." This group, therefore, is most often identified as the actual stigmatizers.

It is important to note here that other work by lesser-known researchers has addressed some groups that were largely ignored in these early days of stigma research and by many mainstream researchers, Durkheim and Goffman included. Later researchers began to recognize and incorporate the insights of these early researchers. For example, Ida B. Wells was known internationally for her fight against the practice of lynching in the United States (Wells-Barnett & Royster, 1997). The common practice of lynching, or the hanging and often shooting and disfigurement of mostly African American men, was the direct outcome of the stigma assigned to African Americans (and occasionally other ethnic groups). This stigma was perpetuated by the institutional systems that supported and later justified the slave trade in the early United States. This devaluation of the lives of African Americans allowed mobs to abduct, torture, and kill individuals for acts such as owning businesses that competed with white-owned businesses, speaking to white women, or attempting to participate in political processes. Charlotte Perkins Gilman (1898), another lesser-known writer, addressed stigma through the lens of gender inequality. Gilman was an early feminist who advocated for equitable recognition of the roles men and women held in society. Although works by writers such as Wells and Gilman are much less well known, they recognized the inherent relationship between stigma and the systems that allow for and support stigmatization, particularly of marginalized groups. Recent work by Tyler and colleagues (Jensen & Tyler, 2015; Tyler, 2018; Tyler & Slater, 2018; Walker, 2008) highlights these exclusions and the importance of recognizing the contributions of early, marginalized researchers.

In the late twentieth century, others began to make important contributions that would pave the way for organizational stigma research. Jones et al. (1984) not only provided an in-depth examination of the types of individuals considered stigmatized but also explored the relationships among the "normal" and "deviant" (or as Goffman called them, the "own"). Although not addressing organizational stigma specifically, Jones, et al. (1984) provided insights on the stigmatization process for those working within clinical settings dealing with the needs of the stigmatized. Stigmatized individuals may carry stigma to other aspects of their life, including the organizations where they work, volunteer, participate, or which they patronize. Consequently, people working within these settings that interact with stigmatized individuals can be impacted.

In the following section, we explore how the foundational insights of Goffman and others led to our contemporary understanding of individual-level stigma in the organizational context.

2.1.1 From Individual Identity to the Organization

Whether the source of stigma is individual or organizational, physical or tribal, concealable or unconcealable, many studies have found that individuals view stigma as an inherent part of their identity. Tyler (2020) particularly noted that, historically, stigma has been carved, sometimes literally, into the bodies of the stigmatized. Slaves, women, the mentally and physically disabled, refugees and others were marked to label them as identifiably "less than" or "other." These marks, often brands, tattoos, or scars but also in the form of collars, masks and muzzles, were historically used to identify and aid in the recapture and retrieval of runaway slaves or prisoners. By permanently marking individuals, the stigma quite literally became a part of their physical identity. The stigma was further imposed through the production of stigmatizing marks, which often took place in public venues so as to reinforce and provide meaning to the marks. This included whipping and flogging during the slave trade or forcing women to wear iron head enclosures with metal bits to restrain them from speaking (Tyler, 2020). These imposed physical marks that identify the stigmatized can encourage physical violence (both in terms of external attacks and self-harm), exclusion, and rejection based on the label associated with the mark.

In management, the identity work literature has examined stigmatized identities of individuals (see Kreiner, Mihelcic, & Mikolon, 2022, for a review). Notably, stigmatized identities are negotiated through numerous social interactions and relationships (Blumer, 1969). These dynamics often take place within organizational contexts. Lyons, Pek, and Wessel (2017) showed how individuals who are member of stigmatized groups use their position within occupations to manage their own stigma and others' perceptions of the stigmatized group. Research on individual stigma has shown how the stigma label defines and shapes the careers and work of individuals within organizations and also how organizations are impacted by the experiences of these individuals (Kreiner & Mihelcic, & Mikolon, 2020; Melton & MacCharles, 2021; Narendra, Reveley, & Almeida, 2021; Van Portfliet, 2022). While that literature is too lengthy and broad to review here in full, an important point is the fact that workers are often stigmatized individuals.

Stigmatized employees are inextricably tied to their identities, and their stigma may influence numerous parts of organizations. For example, one of the most researched areas of study concerns how employees manage their stigmatized identities at work. Research on how employees conceal, reveal, and manage LGBTQ+ identities has implications for human resource and organizational behavior research but also extends to organizational identities and theories (Anteby & Anderson, 2014; Clair, Beatty, & MacLean, 2005; Tilcsik, Anteby, & Knight, 2015; Wiesenfeld, Wurthmann, & Hambrick, 2008). Employee interactions can be affected by concerns over stigma by association among workers who may or may not share the stigmatized identity or wish to conceal their stigmatized identity (Ragins, 2008; Kulik, Bainbridge, & Cregan, 2008; Lauriano & Coacci, 2023; Tilcsik, Anteby, & Knight, 2015). Furthermore, beyond the ways in which individuals' stigmatized identity(ies) can impact an organization, stigma can also be linked to an *organizational* identity. Having a spoiled identity has multiple implications for organizations, impacting various stakeholders, performance measures, and organizational outcomes. For example, stigmas focused on physical taint generally entail a sense of revulsion toward groups of people considered "dirty" (Ashforth,

1999; Douglas, 1966), and these types of stigmas may be aggregated to the organizations that support groups of people with physical taint, such as substance use treatment.

In addition to the negative aspects of stigmatized identity in organizational contexts, recent work has also focused on how stigmatized identities can be helpful in constructing safe spaces for stigmatized practices and industry categories. Having a shared identity can allow for the stigmatized to construct and advocate for their collective group. Research has shown that individuals within stigmatized occupations may work to reinforce a stigma hierarchy based on internally created distinctions within a stigmatized setting and the safe spaces that a shared identity can sometimes encourage may be more nuanced than a stigma-free haven that researchers previously thought (Toubiana & Ruebottom, 2022).

Thus, research on individual stigma has many implications for research at higher levels of analysis. As the flow of stigma can be multidirectional, stigma can be transferred between individuals and organizations. Individual identities are often permeated by organizational attributes and vice versa. Next, we expound on one of the most valuable areas of research on the complex interaction between individual stigma and organizational dynamics.

2.1.2 Stigma as a Component of Occupational Identity

One area in management research related to stigma research that encompasses aspects of stigmatized identities is the research on dirty work. Dirty work entails continued and pervasive association with work that is physically, morally or socially tainted and perceived by society as "visceral repugnance" (Ashforth & Kreiner, 1999: 415; Douglas, 1966). What qualifies as dirty work is highly subjective. Occupations such as garbage collection, animal butchering, and funeral services are typically necessary and important parts of daily life, but they are perceived as dirty work. "Dirty workers" may also be considered heroes, such as in the case of healthcare professionals during the recent pandemic (Glerum, 2021).

Drawing from social psychology and identity work literatures, the dirty work literature has dealt with issues that range from how groups of dirty workers internalize and cope with the work they do and how that work is perceived by a society that needs or wants it, but avoids or demeans those who do it (Ashforth & Kreiner, 1999). Specifically, dirty workers experience stigma as a result of their association with an occupation or work that is deemed unseemly in some way. This leads to dirty workers experiencing stigma in the form of devaluation, low esteem, and deindividuation, as in the case of butchers (Simpson et al.,

2014), as well as feelings of marginalization to the point of being completely ignored, as in the case of cleaners (van Vlijmen, 2019). Ashforth and colleagues (2007) showed that managers in certain professions are acutely aware of stigma assigned to their own occupations, and are affected by stigma through increased role complexity and the need for active stigma management, both internally and externally. Other research has shown that dirty workers may manage stigma by building a support system where they have a sense of belonging (Ashforth & Kreiner, 1999; Kreiner, Ashforth, & Sluss, 2006; Toubiana & Ruebottom, 2022). Cognitive experiences may involve the negotiation of one's own identity or sensemaking around the work or organization (Hamilton, Redman, & McMurray, 2019). Ashforth, Kreiner, and Sluss (2006) also discussed how internal stakeholders of stigmatized organizations experience stigma differently depending on whether the stigma is central to their occupation or incidental.

In their various studies, Ashforth and Kreiner and their colleagues specifically label the social evaluation of this work as stigma and stigmatizing, though the focus of that stigma is on the workers themselves and their occupation at the individual-level of analysis. While they do not address the stigmatization of the organizations in which the work is done, they clearly link the stigmatization of the work to generalized negative social evaluations of the types of organizations and industries engaged in that work.

Although research on organizational stigma and dirty work is often grouped together, stark differences between the two exist. Most notably, most dirty work research is based on individual-level variables, focused on the work and the worker. The work being done may or may not be part of an organization. In her influential work, Mary Douglas (1966) identified numerous types of dirty work that included unpaid work at home, such as cleaning or childcare, often associated with the roles of women or children. Toubiana and Ruebottom (2022) have shown how internal dynamics within a stigmatized profession can lead to individual-level differences in their ranks and group hierarchies.

In the next section, we turn our focus to organizational stigma and specifically discuss the permeability of stigma between individual and organizational levels, and highlighting the similarities and differences between individual stigma and organizational stigma.

2.2 The Permeability of Stigma across Levels

The interplay between individual stigma and organizational stigma has implications for several different areas of management research. For example, the stigma associated with disability may mean that organizations are less likely to hire workers with some disabilities due to concerns that hiring them may also lead to organizational stigma. Specifically, due to the negative associations with non-concealable disabilities, organizations may have concerns that such workers are more expensive or troublesome than those without such disabilities (Hernandez et al., 2008). Also, customers might forego doing business with the organization due to discomfort when dealing with such disabled employees (Vickers, 2015). This also applies to other types of stigma. For example, Dean (2010, 2011) found that some customers assumed that tattooed employees are not intelligent or trustworthy. These assumptions might lead organizations to forego hiring employees with visible tattoos, particularly in service-oriented jobs (Timming et al., 2017), to prevent potential negative impacts on their business due to customer concerns. On the organizational side, when dealing with issues related to individual-level stigma, companies that adopt LGBTQ+-inclusive policies (Gardberg et al., 2002) such as Disney have been repeatedly boycotted and legally targeted because of their friendly policies toward LGBTQ+ groups, including offering insurance benefits to same-sex partners of their employees and, in the case of Disney, specifically, including gay characters in its television programs and movies.

Organizations that conduct "dirty work" may face multilevel outcomes, both internally and externally. Internally, workers may be stigmatized, suffering from physical and psychological strains (Simpson et al., 2014). Externally, these organizations may face sanctions and isolation from various audiences due to the organizational-level stigma (Tracey & Phillips, 2016). Employees of stigmatized organizations may experience confrontations and social buffering or ostracization, effectively marginalizing them and cutting them off from certain groups or resources (e.g., Tracey & Phillips, 2016). Some of these experiences can be self-imposed or externally imposed. Frandsen and Morsing (2022) found that individual workers may use emotional detachment to manage their work when an organization experiences a scandal.

Thus, stigma can flow in different directions, making it important to distinguish individual-level stigma and organizational-level stigma. In the next section, we outline some of the similarities and differences between these individual-level foundations and how they might be confused with, inform, and underlie our understanding of organizational stigma.

2.2.1 Similarities and Differences between Individual and Organizational Stigma

There are clear similarities between individual stigma and organizational stigma. Because stigma is a social evaluation, it is a socio-cognitive process that requires collective-level agreement about the discreditable attribute(s) by stigmatizing audiences, and it can be internalized by those who are stigmatized, whether the stigmatized are individuals or collectives. In other words, both are the result of audience or public social evaluations that define attributes, behaviors, or characteristics as flawed or discredited. Both levels of stigma can also have negative outcomes, including economic losses, social impediments, legal sanctions, and even negative survival outcomes. For example, tribal stigmas have long been used to keep people of certain ethnicities or genders from employment and have been associated with organizational losses based on support for or employment of members of those groups. For example, violence against LGBTQ+ individuals has been the cause of untold deaths within that population, and violence against organizations can harm workers, patrons, investors, and bystanders (Herek, 1998).

Devers et al. (2009) identified three important dimensions that exist for both individual and organizational stigma but are manifested very differently at each level. These dimensions are: (1) types of stigmatizing conditions, (2) how preventable or removable stigma is, and (3) how pervasive the stigma is. As discussed previously, individuals are stigmatized based on character, physical, and tribal attributes. These conditions do not translate clearly to the organizational level; however, there may be some imperfect corollaries.

In terms of the types of stigmatizing conditions, organizational character attributes may include scandals or organizational failures (Sutton & Callahan, 1987), while the equivalent to tribal stigma may come from organizational or product characteristics, such as corporate ownership (Tsui-Auch et al., 2022) or ingredients. Physical attributes may reflect physical facilities and the activities that occur there, as in butcher shops or nuclear power plants (Piazza & Perretti, 2015).

Moreover, individuals typically do not have the influence or ability to alter audiences' perceptions of their discreditable attributes (Toubiana, 2020). Organizations, on the other hand, often have more agency in managing stigma. Although many organizations are stigmatized based on the stigma of individuals involved in the organization (Savio, 2017), other organizations are assigned stigma due to their policies, practices, customers, or product category (Hudson, 2008; Hudson & Okhuysen, 2009; Vergne, 2012). Organizational stigma can be lessened using impression management techniques (Elsbach & Sutton, 1992) and stigma management activities (Hampel & Tracey, 2017; Hudson & Okhuysen, 2009; Piazza & Perretti, 2015; Wolfe & Blithe, 2015). Organizations (and certain individuals, such as celebrities) can enact media or public relations campaigns to alter the ways they are viewed by audiences, both those that stigmatize the organization (Devers et al., 2009; Elsbach & Sutton, 1992; Hudson, 2008;

Hudson & Okhuysen, 2009) and those that support it (Campana, Duffy, & Micheli, 2022; Helms & Patterson, 2014; Ruebottom et al., 2022).

Finally, the pervasiveness of the stigma is highly dependent upon the stigmatizing condition, such as the type of event leading to stigma. This dimension varies highly based on the level of analysis for numerous reasons, including, but not limited to, the possibility of accountability, and the concealability of the condition (i.e., bankruptcy versus partnering with suppliers who engage in child labor; white-collar crime versus violent crime). All stigmas are culturally determined and therefore have some level of variability in pervasiveness; however, individual stigma has a higher degree of consistency across contexts. For example, people who are differently abled (disabled) may be protected by laws in one context and not another, but the individual cognitive and emotional responses to disabilities remain fairly consistent across contexts and cultures.

To sum up, this section discusses key insights from stigma research prior to the emergence of organizational stigma and examines how these insights shape our understanding of organizational stigma. In the next section, we delve into the literature on organizational stigma and illustrate how our understanding of it has evolved.

3 The Development of Stigma Theory

While the important work on individual-level stigma provides some of the foundations for examinations of organizational stigma, the translation across levels is neither direct nor simple. To help facilitate this transition, we begin with a historical review of the ways in which stigma research was translated to an understanding of certain types of organizations, then identify the creation and eventual establishment of organizational stigma research. Our intent is to show how stigma research has progressed from a broad understanding of stigma as an individual-level consideration to stigma as an organizational experience and attribute.

3.1 Introducing a New School of Thought

The foundations for the study of stigmatized organizations were laid over decades using a variety of labels to describe what we now think of as stigmatized organizations. Everett C. Hughes (1984), in a lecture given in 1951, discussed the existence of what he termed bastard institutions, meaning the organizations that served socially disapproved populations or made activities that were otherwise deemed taboo possible. He gave prostitution as an example of such a bastard institution.

Although Hughes's comments were given little attention at the time, some years later, a group of scholars working with Robert Sutton at Stanford University began to focus on the phenomenon of stigmatized organizations and practices in the 1980s. Sutton and Callahan (1987) built on Goffman's (1963) seminal work to analyze several instances of corporate bankruptcy and the stigmatization of both the bankrupt firms and their management and employees. Their work was the first to apply the label of stigma to organizations and the attributes of organizations, providing a strong intellectual basis for further examinations of the phenomenon. Similarly, Ginzel, Kramer, and Sutton (1992) analyzed the roles played by alternative and sometimes competing audiences of a firm that suffered from making available a product that was perceived by some to be defective and dangerous, in this case, silicone breast implants. The stigmatization of the firm lasted for years, causing it to attempt to manage these multiple audiences through a variety of impression management techniques. While not focusing on the stigmatization of the firm, per se, their analysis was of the organizational and audience responses to that stigma.

In a truly groundbreaking study, Elsbach and Sutton (1992) studied two activist organizations that used highly controversial actions (e.g., disruption of a service at a Cathedral, office takeovers, and tree spiking) to draw attention to their areas of activism and then used impression management techniques to manage the stigma they had drawn to themselves. Their work was innovative in a number of ways. First, the organizations and the actions they studied were well outside of the mainstream topic matter traditionally examined in management and organization journals. Second, the authors provided one of the first studies of how organizations knowingly engage in actions that might be stigmatized in order to achieve their goals. Finally, the study also provided insights into how organizations may intentionally manage the ways in which their actions are perceived by external audiences. While not using the label of organizational stigma, their work laid additional foundations for the study of stigmatized organizations due to the controversial nature of the organizations and organizational actions studied.

In another highly innovative study, Dutton and Dukerich (1991) examined the case of a regional transportation agency suffering from stigma transfer due to a stigmatized subset of the users, the homeless, of their space. Their study followed the progression of challenges the agency faced and changes it engaged in as they sought to both provide services to the homeless and to manage and lessen the stigmatization of that subset and of the agency itself. Once again, Dutton and Dukerich (1991) did not apply the label of stigma to either the agency or its users, but like Elsbach and Sutton (1992), they helped to provide the basis for studying stigmatized organizations through their choice of subject and their conceptualization of how such organizations respond. This led the way for others to address how organizations manage stigma and thrive in such settings, whether the stigma be that of their clients (Tracey & Phillips, 2016), core practices (Hudson & Okhuysen, 2009; Helms & Patterson, 2014), categories (Ruebottom, et al., 2022; Toubiana & Ruebottom, 2022; Vergne, 2012) or markets (Slade-Shantz et al., 2019; Tsui-Auch, et al, 2022).

3.2 The Development of Organizational Stigma Research

3.2.1 The Emergence of Organizational Stigma Research

Motivated in part by the groundbreaking work of Elsbach and Sutton (1992), Hudson (2008) offered a conceptual paper arguing that stigmatized organizations deserved further attention. He made a distinction in the nature of the stigma experienced by organizations between "event stigma" and "core stigma" (see Section 3.3.2). Hudson also differentiated core stigma from other forms of social evaluations and discussed its sources and outcomes. He went on to discuss strategic responses that core stigmatized firms might deploy.

Devers et al. (2009) introduced what they called a "general theory" for the study of stigmatized organizations. They noted the importance of studying stigmatized organizations due to the prevalence of stigma in organizations and the lack of attention that it had received. They too went on to delineate stigma from other forms of social evaluation of organizations, and, as we mentioned before, they identified the similarities and differences between individual-level stigma and organization-level stigma. They also examined the labeling theory to capture the stigma emergence process and its outcomes.

Since the publication of these two calls for the study of stigma, many have responded by engaging in empirical studies of both forms of stigma and related negative social evaluation. This was when the theory development of organizational stigma began. Several important studies emerged during this time. Next, we discuss these works by focusing on the variety of settings studied, the processes of stigmatization, and the responses that stigmatized organizations have been found to engage in to lessen or ameliorate that stigma.

3.2.2 Settings

Diverse, unique empirical settings are one of the hallmarks of stigma research. Most of the empirical work on stigmatized organizations has focused on core stigma. Empirical studies of event-stigmatized organizations have focused on individual firms and generally fall under the heading of organizational misconduct or scandal. These studies rarely use the label of stigma (see Greve, Palmer, & Pozner, 2010 for a review).

Studies of core-stigmatized organizations have looked at a variety of settings ranging from whole industries to individual organizations. For example, Davidson (1996), although he did not use the label of stigma but instead referred to the industries he examined as "sin industries," studied the US tobacco, firearms, alcohol, gambling, and pornography industries. Similarly, Galvin, Ventresca, and Hudson (2004) did a comparative analysis of the gaming and tobacco industries in the United States. Helms and Patterson (2014) examined the mixed martial arts (MMA) industry, while Hudson and Okhuysen (2009) studied the industry of men's bathhouses in the United States. Jensen (2010) chose the Danish pornography industry for his study, while Tibbals (2013) chose the US pornography industry. Wolfe and Blithe (2015) examined the legal brothel industry in Nevada, USA, and similarly Ruebottom, Toubiana, and colleagues have studies aspects of sex work (Ruebottom, et al., 2022; Toubiana & Ruebottom, 2022). Roulet (2015) examined the financial services industry in the UK. Piazza and Perretti (2015) examined the US nuclear power industry. Anteby (2010), though not focusing on stigmatized organizations per se, examined the evolution and moral contestation within the New York state market for medical cadavers. Vergne (2012) and Durand and Vergne (2015) examined the global armaments industry. The range of industry settings that this partial listing represents, from traditional sin industries, as defined in the foundational literature on stigma, to more widely accepted, traditional settings for management and organizational scholarship, such as financial firms, demonstrates the wide application of organizational stigma, as well as the potential for future studies of this phenomenon.

Fewer studies have examined a single firm as the setting for understanding the dynamics of organizational stigma. Yue, Rao, and Ingram (2013) examined the retailer Walmart in the United States, while Tracey and Phillips (2016) examined a social service agency, Keystone, in the UK stigmatized due to serving migrants, just one set of their clients. Hampel and Tracey (2017) examined the Cook Travel Agency in the 1800s, the very first travel agency in the world, and hence the founder of today's global industry, which faced intense stigmatization at that time. While the studies of core stigmatized firms have primarily focused on industries, these studies of single organizations show the potential for further examinations of a single in-depth case to yield important insights.

3.2.3 Methodologies

Stigma is causally ambiguous and rarely dyadic, meaning that stigmatizing audiences are more often plural, rather than unitary. Besides the occurrence of stigmatizing events, such as scandals, accidents, and bankruptcies, stigma can stem from objections to an organization's customers, both core practices (as in the case of abortion clinics) and peripheral practices (for example, through the violation of manufacturing ethics), products, industry segments, and associations. Stigma involves multiple stakeholders and audiences, ranging from institutional owners to social action groups to individual customers, advocates, and opponents. For these reasons, stigma research necessitates a deep understanding of the causes of the stigma, the perspectives of the stigmatizing audience or audiences, and the objectives of the stigmatized. These deep levels of understanding almost always necessitate time- and/or space-dependent analysis that encompasses rich data and often at least some qualitative analysis. Indeed, much of stigma research has been longitudinal and included qualitative components. Even those studies involving quantitative analysis provide some qualitative analysis of archival texts to clarify the context and situation of the stigmatized firms under consideration (see for example Durand & Vergne, 2015; Piazza & Perretti, 2015; Vergne, 2012).

One particular challenge for studies of organizational stigma is that of showing that the phenomenon being studied is actually stigmatized. As stigma and other social evaluations are highly culturally determined and as organizations carrying stigma might operate in different industries, countries, or cultures or be involved in various disruptive practices (Ashforth & Kreiner, 1999), there is no universal standard for capturing stigma in empirical contexts. Furthermore, it is worth noting that evidence of organizations suffering from negative outcomes is not sufficient to demonstrate stigma. In other words, neither legislation nor negative outcomes alone can translate to stigma directly. They only reflect some social control agencies' attitudes toward the organization.

So far, most studies on organizational stigma use inductive, qualitative research methods, relying on various types of data, including, but not limited to, archival data, observation, and interview (e.g., Cowden et al., 2022; Hampel & Tracey, 2017; Hudson & Okhuysen, 2009; Tracey & Phillips, 2016). For example, Lashley and Pollock (2020: 441) focused on the stigma of a group of organizations working in the marijuana industry and use longitudinal data from various sources to understand the core stigma reduction process. To demonstrate the existence of stigma, the authors list the key historical events (e.g., "cannabis used medically" and "Controlled Substances Act") that have influenced audiences' evaluations of an organization or group of organizations, as well as the associated labels (e.g., "medicine," "gateway drug" and "killer of motivation") that have emerged during this process. This approach unpacks the cultural background and shows how certain attributes become negatively evaluated due to changes in the social environment (Kipping & Üsdiken, 2014). Similarly, Hampel and Tracey (2017) relied on historical records such as press articles and scholarly sources to construct a longitudinal, rich dataset to investigate destigmatization process of Thomas Cook's travel agency in Victorian Britain. They demonstrate the organizational stigma by developing a detailed account to explain the historical background and discourses regarding class structure and why an organization serving the working class and the lower middle class was stigmatized by the upper middle class and the upper class, with evidence such as quotes from establishment newspapers.

In some other qualitative studies, although they adopt similar methods to address their research questions, organizational stigma is demonstrated through capturing audiences' perception directly. For example, except for using discourse to explain why organizations were stigmatized in the first place, Hudson and Okhuysen (2009) quantified and ranked the institutional environments in which the organizations operated to indicate audiences' perception, collecting archival data and ranking local communities' attributes toward homosexuality based on for example, state and local laws and voting records. Similarly, one type of evidence used to demonstrate stigma by Helms and Patterson (2014) was the number of newspaper articles using stigmatizing labels to describe MMA and related organizations chronologically.

Piazza and Augustine (2022) used fuzzy-set qualitative comparative analysis to examine how patterns of opposition and support from various stakeholders and audiences affect organizational survival. They demonstrate stigma by quantifying several indicators of stigma related to abortion, including anti-abortion legislation, political opposition to abortion, and strengthening of anti-abortion activism.

A few studies also adopted quantitative methods or mixed methods. For example, Vergne (2012) used a mixed-methods approach that includes both a qualitative field research to understand audiences' perceptions and also longitudinal quantitative data to test their hypotheses. The author used content analysis to code the number of disapproving statements in newspapers about arm dealers based on a customized dictionary as a way to measure stigma. Barlow, Verhaal, and Hoskins (2018) demonstrated product category stigma by using online review ratings in the craft beer industry and used it as the main data source to test their hypotheses. Both of these are excellent examples of the use of quantitative data situated within a rich empirical context.

3.3 Theory Development in Organizational Stigma

3.3.1 Negative Consequences

Stigma is generally viewed as a negative phenomenon, given its many adverse implications (Helms & Patterson, 2014). When an organization is marked as deviant, it often faces ostracism, strong disapproval, and public shaming from both external and internal audiences as they try to bring the organization back into alignment with societal norms and values (Devers et al., 2009; Hudson, 2008; Tracey & Phillips, 2016). While it is worth noting that stigma can also have positive implications, such as increasing acceptance from audiences (Campana et al., 2022: 1; Cowden et al., 2022; Helms & Patterson, 2014), the overall impact of organizational stigma is typically negative and can present significant challenges to organizations seeking to survive and thrive.

To be specific, first, Devers et al. (2009) highlighted that organizational stigma reduces stakeholder groups' interactions with the organization as interactions pose the risk of 'stigma transfer'. That is, previously non-stigmatized organizations can be targeted and punished by audiences due to their association with a stigmatized organization (Kulik, Bainbridge, & Cregan, 2008). Empirical evidence suggests that stigmatized organizations can suffer both informal sanctions, such as media attacks (Durand & Vergne, 2015) and negative reactions from employees, customers, and investors (Hudson, 2008; Vergne, 2012; Voss, 2015), and formal sanctions, such as legal sanctions and closure (Hudson & Okhuysen, 2009; Sutton & Callahan, 1987). For example, Durand and Vergne (2015) have shown that diversified organizations with assets in stigmatized categories may divest from the stigmatized industry due to media attacks targeting either the organization or the industry category, which can result in stakeholders reducing or entirely removing support for the stigmatized organization. Pizza and Perretti (2015) have shown that parent organizations with significant involvement in stigmatized categories may become more centrally identified with the stigmatized category, which can make further diversification efforts difficult (Phillips, Turco, & Zuckerman, 2013).

The organizational stigma not only harms the organization itself, but also its insiders. For example, Sutton and Callahan (1987) and Wiesenfeld et al. (2008) found that senior managers and members of the board of directors may suffer negative social and professional consequences, such as social ostracism and difficulty finding new positions or directorships, due to their affiliation with a stigmatized firm. Pozner (2008) has also demonstrated that people will sever ties with organizational elites in stigmatized organizations, leading to decreased career opportunities for these individuals. Hudson and Okhuysen (2009) found that suppliers, regulators, and customers may also suffer negative effects from their association with stigmatized firms.

3.3.2 Event and Core Stigma

Organizational stigma has been mainly characterized as falling into two major categories: event stigma and core stigma (Hudson, 2008). Event stigma is the result of an organizational anomaly such as an accident, a discrete occurrence of misconduct, a scandal, or some other form of episodic event that results in stigmatization. Examples of this type of stigma include instances of corporate and financial fraud (Carberry & King, 2012; Marcel & Cowen, 2014), as well as product defects and recalls (Zavyalova et al., 2012). While many studies of organizational stigma have examined event stigma, these have typically been examined using the theoretical lens of organizational misconduct (Greve et al., 2010; MacLean & Behnam, 2010; Moore, Stuart, & Pozner, 2010), or of challenges to organizational legitimacy (Benner & Ranganathan, 2012; Cavender, Gray, & Miller, 2010; Cowen & Marcel, 2011; Desai, 2011; Jonsson, Greve, & Fujiwara-Greve, 2009; Marcel & Cowen, 2014; Patriotta, Gond, & Schultz, 2011). In recent years, event stigma resulting from scandals due to a variety of actions has become more prevalent, linking the two constructs of stigma and scandal. Of the two forms of stigma, event stigma is more recoverable, more easily eroded, and more easily managed. We discuss some of these management processes in a later section.

The second type of stigma is labeled core stigma, defined as "an evaluation held and often expressed by some social audience(s) that an organization or set of organizations is discounted, discredited, and/or tainted in some way owing to some core attribute or attributes"[2] (Hudson, 2008: 154). Core stigma is, by its nature, inseparable from the organization. The activities that are stigmatized are part of the core business, such as with legal brothels (Wolfe & Blithe, 2015), pornography or exotic dancing (Wry, Lounsbury, & Glynn, 2011), or entrepreneurial ventures in the sex trade (Ruebottom & Toubiana, 2017).

Empirical evaluations of core stigma have looked at its implications, management, sources, and uses in a variety of contexts and situations. For example, Hudson and Okhuysen (2009) examined men's bathhouses to find how stigmatized organizations avoid isolation from stakeholders through boundary management techniques. Durand and Vergne (2015) and Vergne (2012) examined global arms manufacturers and found that organizations manage their business portfolios to divest of units included in a stigmatized industry. Helms and Patterson (2014) examined MMA organizations in the United States and found that these firms balanced state-level licensing requirements with maintaining a transgressive, stigmatized image. Hampel and Tracey (2017) examined the case of Cook's Travel Agency and found that the organization was able

---

[2] Importantly, in the first conceptualization of core stigma, the concept was characterized by the first author of this Element as being a strong form of moral illegitimacy, the opposite pole from legitimacy on a single dimension. The author no longer believes that to be correct and has joined others to make the argument that these are distinct social evaluations (Ashforth, 2019; Devers & Mishina, 2019; Helms et al., 2019; Patterson, Hudson, & Helms, 2019).

to de-stigmatize its core operations over time through impression management and communications techniques. Barlow, Verhaal, and Hoskins (2018) have examined how, within the craft beer industry, participation in a stigmatized product category had negative spillover effects for the other, related products in a firm's product portfolio, decreasing the organization's overall value among relevant audience members in general. These are just a small sample of the studies that have emerged examining this form of organizational stigma.

When examining stigmatized industries and organizations within them, some authors have chosen to use the label "categorical stigma," capturing the stigma at the collective level instead of organizational level, such as global arms manufacturers (Vergne, 2012), nuclear energy power plants (Piazza & Perretti, 2015), or, within the craft beer brewers, lager beers (Barlow, Verhaal, & Hoskins, 2018). The firms in the categories can be targeted due to their core attributes shared within these categories. Indeed, for most core-stigmatized organizations, all the firms in that category are similarly stigmatized if these categories are salient to audiences.

However, individual firms within a category may be core stigmatized for being seen as a part of another category. For instance, TikTok is a social media company that is currently being stigmatized for being owned by a Chinese firm. Similarly, X (formerly Twitter) is a social media company currently stigmatized due to the actions of its new owner, Elon Musk. While social media firms are as a whole are not core stigmatized (at least not by large segments of the public), these firms appear to be so due to other reasons.

3.3.3 Degree of Stigma

Organizations suffer different degrees of organizational stigma, which mainly depends on the relative distance between the attributes of the organization and the values, beliefs, and ideologies of the evaluating audience (Hudson, 2008). To be specific, social evaluations in general are based on a "socially constructed system of norms, values, beliefs, and definitions" (Suchman, 1995: 574) held in common by the evaluating audience. When there is a lack of congruence, a difference, or a contradiction between the values of the audience and the evaluated attributes of the organization, this leads an audience to evaluate the organization or set of organizations negatively. Yet not all such differences or contradictions are of equal magnitude or distance. For example, most people probably evaluate the core work of garbage collection agencies negatively (Ashforth & Kreiner, 1999). Yet most also recognize the necessity of that work and so merely try to avoid interacting with organizational employees – specifically, those doing the actual waste collection – or even thinking about them more than strictly necessary. On the other hand, many people in the United States strenuously object to abortion service providers (Brulliard, 2003; Simonds, 1996) and so seek to interrupt or stop their operations, because they do not perceive that work as necessary, despite it often being lifesaving. Furthermore, organizations that carry stigma can be supported and even celebrated by other groups of stakeholders or audiences due to their different values and beliefs. These organizations exist at the nexus of multiple social audiences, some stigmatizing, some not, contesting the social evaluation and appropriateness of the organization or industry (Hudson, 2008).

In each of these cases, the degree of negative perception points to a difference in the degree of stigma, with the distance between the values and beliefs of the audience members being greater in the case of abortion service providers than in the case of the garbage collection agencies. These perceptions may vary not only among organizations but among and even within audiences. For example, alcohol use may be highly stigmatized among certain audiences but even within those audiences, there may be varying degrees of stigma. The degree of stigma also depends on whether these values, beliefs, and ideologies are salient and relevant during a certain period of time (Hilgartner & Bosk, 1988). For example, firms may carry a stronger stigma for violating data privacy now than they did twenty years ago.

3.3.4 Stigmatization

Stigma as an outcome has been well defined, but the process of stigmatization has not been as thoroughly examined. Stigmatization refers to the social process of enacting and manifesting the negative social evaluation of stigma (Pescosolido & Martin, 2015). We take the position that "all organizations or populations are stigmatized by some audiences at some time" (Hudson, 2008: 263). However, it is important to note that an organization suffering stigmatization from some audiences does not necessarily have the attribute of stigma; this occurs only when such negative evaluation is persistent and self-sustaining (Devers et al., 2009). Unlike stigma, stigmatization focuses on the processes and practices that ostracize or isolate organizations or that prompt them to adopt preferred or socially acceptable patterns of behavior (e.g., exiting the stigmatized industry, discontinuing disruptive behaviors). The expressions of stigmatization by different audiences vary. As Ashforth and Kreiner (1999) have pointed out, stigma entails a "visceral repugnance" to the discreditable attribute or behavior. The expressions of this repugnance range from avoidance, to mild expressions of disapproval such as scowls or frowns, to strong expressions such as a letter to the editor of the local paper or trade publication, to picketing, to even stronger expressions such as boycotts and even bomb and death threats (Hudson, 2008).

Most of the current studies focus on stigmatization during the phase of stigma emergence (Galvin, Ventresca, & Hudson, 2004; Lashley & Pollock, 2020). It is often discussed as a process of labeling. Wiesenfeld and colleagues (2008) illustrated how stigma arises from a declaration of corporate failure, where arbiters assign blame and disseminate their judgments and interpretations. Devers et al. (2009) highlighted a two-stage model that involves an individual-level process of perceiving generalized value incongruence with the target organization and vilifying it, and then a social process that aggregates the collective perceptions and vilification toward the target organization. These studies highlight two key labeling processes: how an organization becomes tainted as a whole, and how negative evaluations disseminate across various audiences until a consensus is reached. In an empirical study, Wang and colleagues (2021) provided empirical evidence of how the medical profession in China moved from collective approval toward stigma through a labeling process. The second moment of stigmatization focuses on audiences' actions and enactments toward well-established organizational stigma, such as rhetorical and material practices triggered by stigma transfer that exert impact on organizations involved (Dong et al., 2023).

The degree of stigmatization can be impacted by the level of awareness that evaluating audiences have of the organization and its stigmatizing attributes. Stigmatized organizations often attempt to conceal their stigmatized attributes or even their entire operations and location as much as possible to avoid negative attention (Hudson & Okhuysen, 2009). In other cases, stigmatized organizations may publicize their stigmatized attributes strategically in order to attract attention and resources (Helms & Patterson, 2014). Some audiences may be unaware of the organization's stigmatized attributes and therefore may not act against it. However, others who are more acutely aware, perhaps due to the discrepancy between the nature of the organization and their own values and beliefs, may choose to take action against the organization.

For example, most consumers of meat and meat products are largely unaware, except perhaps in the vaguest sense, of the operations and routines of slaughter houses (Jarvis, Goodrick & Hudson, 2019) and thus are unlikely to take action against the firms that produce their food. However, those who are aware of these processes and object strongly may take action to raise public awareness and pressure the firms to change their practices. Thus, the greater the awareness of negatively evaluating audiences of the existence and stigmatized attributes of the organization or set of organizations, the more likely it is that action by those audiences will lead to greater degree of stigmatization.

The degree of stigmatization can also be impacted by the relative power of the audience or stakeholders doing the stigmatization (Hudson, 2008). Powerful audiences have greater ability to stigmatize through their political power and social influence, with both factors being highly interrelated. These audiences have access to political actors and can control the spread of their stigmatizing message through various media outlets (Clemente & Roulet, 2015). Additionally, high-status audiences often seek to limit the influence of organizations or practices that pose a threat to their standing by stigmatizing them (Magee & Galinsky, 2008). The power of such audiences is sometimes related to their size or dominant position, with larger audiences being able to exercise power more effectively than smaller or marginalized ones. Audiences with greater power and influence are more likely to use their power to disrupt or shut down a stigmatized firm. In some cases, less powerful actors may seek to mobilize more powerful audiences to cause such disruptions. For example, Helms and Patterson (2014) have shown how a relatively small number of individuals from medicine, politics, and sport were able to mobilize strong opposition to the practice of MMA, effectively prohibiting the practice from appearing on television and any other profitable outlets. However, the authors also showed how the relatively small population of MMA promoters and practitioners were able to motivate supportive audiences to continue engaging in the practice at least partially by emphasizing the shared desire among practitioners to challenge the audiences that opposed the practice and the strong identities associated with it.

3.3.5 Experienced Stigma

While stigma or stigmatizing activities targeting an organization reflect on audiences' perception and their actions, experienced organizational stigma, like felt stigma at the individual level, provides a lens that encourages scholars to pay attention to target organizations themselves. Experienced stigma pertains to how the organization, its internal processes and members are impacted by stigma or stigmatization activities. Importantly, stigmatization activities conducted by audiences or the stigma held by audiences toward the organization do not necessarily translate into experienced stigma to the extent that organizations may need to react. Experienced stigma of organizations depends on how organizations and their members interpret the external audiences' perception and stigmatization activities, and whether they suffer from these perceptions and activities. These can be manifested through internal dynamics at both individual and collective levels, including roles and identity (Jones & King, 2014), daily practices, group dynamics, and strategy formulation, which goes beyond the external manifestations of stigma such as stock price and sales decrease. For instance, Tracey and Phillips (2016) identified various ways in which organizational members experienced stigma due to their organization's support of immigrant populations, including identity crisis. They focused on how the organization discussed the stigma assigned to it and how it managed and interpreted the stigma. Frandsen and Morsing (2022) showed that frontline employees felt stigmatized due to event stigma not only when interacting with customers but also with friends and family, and some of them detached their emotions to minimize the emotionally damaging effects and to protect their identity from threats.

So far, experienced stigma has received limited attention compared with stigma and stigmatization. The dirty work literature provides valuable insights into experienced stigma that stigma scholars can leverage. For example, within a stigmatized working environment, individuals can experience stigma through increased role complexity and active stigma management. For example, cognitive experiences may involve the negotiation of one's own identity or sensemaking around the work (Kreiner, Ashforth, & Sluss, 2006) and may vary depending on whether the stigma is central to the organization or incidental. At the collective level, such experienced stigma may manifest in the forms of collective devaluation, low esteem and deindividuation (Simpson et al., 2014), and feelings of extreme marginalization (van Vlijmen, 2019).

3.3.6 Stigma Transfer

Stigma is contagious. That is, it can transfer to another entity due to an association with – or similarity to – stigmatized ones (Hudson & Okhuysen, 2009; Vergne, 2012). When stigma transfers, the previously non-stigmatized entity experiences similar negative consequences as the already stigmatized one. The problem of stigma transfer was first identified by Goffman (1963), who labeled it "courtesy stigma." From an outsider's perspective, those bearing a courtesy stigma "share the taint of the stigma ... are all obliged to share some of the discredit of the stigmatized person to whom they are related" (Goffman, 1963). For example, Pontikes, Negro, and Rao (2010) investigated the impact of stigma transfer on individual members of the entertainment industry during the US government's search for suspected communists in the 1950s. They discovered that the focal artists who had previously worked with fellow artists who were later found to be Communist Party members were stigmatized by association, even though they had worked together before the membership revelation.

Social psychologists have identified two processes that help explain how such transfer happens: automatic, spontaneous negative reactions and cognitive, deliberative reactions (Negro et al., 2021; Pryor et al., 2004). The first process involves unconscious reactions, that is, automatic and implicit negative affective responses. Research shows that stigma transfer at the individual level is rampant (Phelan, Bromet, & Link, 1998). A single exposure to negative social stimuli can be sufficient to produce stigma transfer, because such stimuli are usually salient and powerful, and thus audiences are sensitive to them. Moreover, audiences tend to maintain cognitive consistency "across the yoked targets" (Kulik et al., 2008), meaning that they may extend negative evaluations to other entities that are associated with stigmatized ones. As a result, the target entity may suffer from transferred stigma and experience similar outcomes as the stigmatized one. Meanwhile, a second process involves conscious and explicit reactions that depend on whether audiences are motivated to process further information about that transfer (Kulik et al., 2008). If so, the transferred stigma may be strengthened and become self-sustaining, making it hard to remove. It is important to note that both automatic and deliberative processes can happen simultaneously. Recent research shows that destigmatization effort can facilitate the diminishing of conscious prejudice but the non-conscious prejudices remain, with the result that audiences might be "unaware of their implicit prejudice towards those stigmatized by association" (Negro et al., 2021).

Stigma transfer can occur across different levels. The stigma attached to organizations often transfers to workers or others in the organization and to organizational partners, and vice versa (Zhang et al., 2021). For example, Sutton and Callahan (1987) and Wiesenfeld, Wurthmann, and Hambrick (2008) found that top managers are often stigmatized due to organizational failures or bankruptcy. Mikolon et al. (2016) showed that stigma can transfer from homeless employees to their organizations and from there to non-homeless employees.

At the organizational level, stigma can transfer between actors who share similar traits or characteristics but who may not be associated in any practical way and between actors who are practically associated but dissimilar (Dong et al., 2023). To be specific, first, a stigma source can contaminate a group of similar peers that stigmatizing audiences might generalize discrediting features of an organization to other similar organizations, particularly if they are deemed to be core to these organizations (Paruchuri & Misangyi, 2015; Roulet, 2020; Vergne, 2012; Yu, Sengul, & Lester, 2008). For example, Roulet (2015) demonstrated how organizations in the finance industries suffered from devaluation due to the shared values with other stigmatized organizations. This may occur when the target's interaction with the stigma source makes covert characteristics that are shared with stigma source salient.

To prevent stigma transfer caused by similarities, organizations often dilute audiences' attention to the similarities they share with the stigma source (Durand & Vergne, 2015; Phung et al., 2021; Vergne, 2012; Wolfe & Blithe, 2015), or confront the stigmatization of the core attribute directly (Khessina, Reis, & Verhaal, 2021). For example, Phung et al. (2021) showed how Uber distanced itself from the taint associated with taxi drivers by highlighting its distinctiveness from taxi companies to minimize the attention to the similarities. Durand and Vergne (2015) also showed that organizations experiencing stigmatization are motivated to divest from the stigmatized industry and divert audience's attention from the shared characteristics they have with the industry. Organizations may also deal with the stigma transfer by confronting the stigma directly. For example, Khessina et al. (2021) showed how legal marijuana sellers alleviated customers' concerns of stigma transfer and facilitated the market destigmatization process by publicly advocating their business.

Second, stigma can also transfer from a stigmatized source to a dissimilar, separate entity through an exposed association (Kulik et al., 2008; Pontikes et al., 2010). Associations with stigmatized entities deviate from or transgress socially constructed expectations about the target of the stigma transfer and how that target should act. Different from similarity-based stigma transfer, the targets of association-based stigma transfer do not possess stigmatizing attributes. They are mainly targeted for their relationship with the stigmatized organization. Prior studies show that to minimize the possibility or the effects of the association-based transfer, the previously non-stigmatized organizations may terminate their relationships with the stigmatized entities. Jensen (2006) showed that after the exposure of an accounting firm's scandalous involvement with Enron, the accounting firm's former network partners ended their relationships with them to avoid stigma transfer. When withdrawal from the association is not feasible, organizations might engage with hiding strategies or maintaining their relationships with the source and join in stigma management effort. For example, Hudson and Okhuysen (2009) showed how men's bathhouses buffer their suppliers and regulators from stigma transfer or its effects, and that suppliers and regulators limit the public exposure of their associations for the same purpose. Tracey and Phillips (2016) examined how a social services agency, which suffered from transferred stigma due to serving refugees, challenged the stigma attached to refugees while justifying their engagement with them. This then allowed organizational members to see the organization positively.

3.3.7 Managing Stigma

The empirical examinations of stigmatized organizations have primarily looked at the ways in which stigma is managed. As Greenwood et al. (2017: 5), suggest, when it comes to stigma, organizations hide it, lose it, or use it. In other words, some firms will seek to conceal themselves or the stigmatized attributes of the firm while others will attempt to lessen the stigmatization they face through destigmatization processes. Some firms, however, will not try to conceal or to lessen the stigma they face, but rather will embrace it and use it as a competitive resource. As with any typology, these categories are perhaps analytically convenient, though the findings of studies of organizations often cross or occupy more than one of these. We discuss each category in turn next.

Concealing Stigma. Hudson and Okhuysen (2009) showed that men's bathhouses are often able to manage their stigma by hiding in plain sight. By locating in out-of-the-way industrial sections of cities and limiting external signage and other markers, bathhouses are able to attract core customers while avoiding the notice of more condemning audiences. Hudson and Okhuysen (2009) also found that while these bathhouses advertise in local and sometimes national media targeted to the gay community, even in the advertisements, text and visuals are coded in ways that let customers understand the ads without being explicit about the nature of the business. In this way, both the bathhouses and stakeholders such as customers, regulators, and vendors are at least partially shielded from the effects of stigma.

Vergne (2012) and Durand and Vergne (2015) showed that diversified firms investing in the global arms industry are able to minimize the attention or scrutiny paid to their participation in that contested industry by divesting or reducing their investment. Carberry and King (2012) showed that by adopting accounting-based corporate governance mechanisms, that is, expensing stock options, firms are able to divert attention away from alleged corporate misconduct and fraud. In this way, firms hide the alleged misconduct behind accounting practices thought to increase management accountability by deflecting attention.

Destigmatization. In the case of stigmatization due to an accident or otherwise anomalous event, organizations often can become decoupled from that stigma by engaging in other, positive behaviors, such as issuing corporate social responsibility reports or by distancing stigmatized portions of the organization from concerned stakeholders (Carberry & King, 2012; Grougiou et al., 2016; Jensen, 2006). However, some event stigmas may be more difficult to disassociate from the organization, for example, if the event was especially scandalous. An example of this is the study by Pontikes, Negro, and Rao (2010), who show stigmatization across levels of analysis and demonstrate the long-lasting stigmatization that resulted from being accused of belonging to the Communist Party in the United States. Sometimes, stigmatized practices that create a scandalous event have become so ingrained within the culture of the organization that they are difficult to separate from the organization, making destigmatization difficult or impossible (Gulli, Kohler, & Patriquin, 2007).

Several studies have examined the processes by which firms attempt to lessen the stigmatization of core elements or attributes of the organization. Dutton and Dukerich (1991) found that the New York/New Jersey Transit authority was able to lose its stigma by incorporating additional community services into both its physical structures and organizational practices. Hills, Voronov, and Hinings (2013) found that wine producers in Ontario, Canada, were able to reduce or lose their stigma by adopting rigid conformity to globalized wine industry practices. Tracey and Phillips (2016) found that a social services firm was able to reduce the stigma they experienced due to their work with a set of stigmatized clients by rhetorically reframing both their clients and the work the firm was doing. Hampel and Tracey (2017) similarly showed Cook's Travel Agency was able to lose its stigmatized identity through rhetorically reframing its services as advantageous to both clients and the broader society. Interestingly, Wolfe and Blithe (2015), in their study of Nevada brothels, found that though the brothels sought to conceal themselves from some audiences, they also sought to destigmatize by presenting an alternative, socially positive organizational image.

Embracing or Using Stigma. In some situations, stigma can be leveraged and used by actors as assets. As Elsbach and Sutton (1992) illustrated, some event stigma may be deemed an acceptable cost for moving an organization's agenda forward, particularly if it can be managed through impression management tactics. In their study, they showed how two organizations, ACT-UP and EarthFirst!, leveraged the attention gained from stigmatizing events to advance their respective agendas of changing the treatment of AIDS patients and stopping logging of old growth forests in the United States. Cowden and colleagues (2022) illustrated in the context of Detroit, Michigan, how entrepreneurs utilize the stigma associated with Detroit to create underdog and comeback narratives to reinforce their collective identities and motivate their endeavors.

Other organizations whose core attributes are stigmatized may be able to operate in a niche market or serve a specific audience. Organizations that are driven by strong social value factors, such as Planned Parenthood, GLAD churches, or the American Freedom Party, all in the United States, or the European Conference on Sex Work, Human Rights, Labour and Migration in

Europe, may be willing to tolerate stigma from certain groups that they see as antithetical to their values rather than try to manage or distance themselves from it.

Similarly, some organizations may embrace their stigma in order to appeal to particular audiences or customer groups. Helms and Patterson (2014) found that MMA organizations in the United States were able to use their transgressive and counter-cultural form of fighting to both differentiate themselves from other forms of fighting entertainment such as boxing and wrestling and to appeal to a niche market of viewers interested in these more extreme forms of fighting. In the United States, tattoo parlors often project transgressive organizational images, especially relating themselves to motorcycle gangs. Similarly, vendors of pornography and sex toys may try to project a highly sexualized, and so stigmatized, image of their products and venues. These types of firms embrace being assigned stigma by groups that have opposing values, because it reinforces their own identity for the customers they seek to attract. In contrast, by examining the case of RuPaul's Drag Race, Campana, Duffy, and Micheli (2022) showed intentional effort to normalize stigmatized practices through catching broader audiences' attention and constructing new realities. Similarly, Savio (2017) examined the informal and formal organizations of dumpster diving and explored how organizations can challenge stigma associated with a practice by building a strong network among similar organization or organizations that espouse similar values. These findings provide support for the claim that organizations become more invested in stigmatized categories when they strongly identify with them.

Having discussed some of the outcomes that the study of organizational stigma and stigmatized organizations can provide for organization scholars, we next compare and differentiate stigma from other forms of social evaluations.

4 Stigma in the Context of Other Social Evaluations

We have argued that stigma is a form of social evaluation that is distinct from other similar constructs. Yet it still falls under the umbrella designation of a social evaluation. Social evaluations represent shared socio-cognitive beliefs and perceptions about organizations (Bitektine, 2011; Devers et al., 2009; Pollock et al., 2019). Social evaluations share certain properties, most notably in the external nature of their creation and assignment. Although social evaluations can be influenced by several different organizational behaviors, the responsibility and control over social evaluations are largely up to external audiences and their perceptions of organizations, within the context of industry and category norms and organizational behaviors. Another important indicator of social evaluations is audience size and significance (Zavyalova, Bundy, & Humphrey, 2022). Relevant audiences may differ depending on the types of social evaluations being examined, but most researchers agree that social evaluations must be shared among a "critical mass" of stakeholders (Devers et al., 2009) or a small group of powerful stakeholders (Pfarrer et al., 2008) for them to impact an organization.

Early social evaluation management research focused largely on the benefits of positive social evaluations (Aldrich & Fiol, 1994; Fombrun & Shanley, 1990; Podolny, 1993; Rindova, Pollock, & Hayward, 2006). More recently, research has provided more nuanced assessments of these benefits, along with insights into the negative side of social evaluation. For example, Suddaby, Bitektine, and Haack (2017) discussed the ways in which legitimacy is a prerequisite factor for successful organizations. Bitektine's (2011) reviewed legitimacy, status, and reputation providing further support for their positive nature, as well as the negative outcomes associated with illegitimacy, bad reputation, and low status.

Whereas most social evaluations can be either positive or negative, stigma is unique in that it "register[s] only on the negative side of the social evaluation spectrum" (Devers et al., 2009: 154). Although this is a major difference between stigma and many other social evaluations, it is not the only one. Furthermore, as stated previously, most organizations sit at the nexus of diverse audiences and are therefore exposed to varying types of evaluations (Hsu & Grodal, 2021; Piazza & Augustine, 2022). Thus, it is important to understand the unique features of each social evaluation. Next, we explicate the specific differences between stigma and some of the related social evaluations, including legitimacy, reputation, status, celebrity, and social disapproval.

4.1 Legitimacy

Legitimacy, or, more accurately, illegitimacy, is likely the concept that is most commonly confused with stigma. In his foundational categorization of legitimacy, Suchman defined it as a "generalized perception or assumption that the actions of an entity are desirable, proper or appropriate within some socially constructed system of norms, values, beliefs and definitions" (Suchman, 1995). Suchman's definition of moral legitimacy provided an early foundation for stigma research and has caused some confusion between the concept of stigma and illegitimacy. Others have expanded on the basic definition, as has Suchman himself, to identify different categories, dimensions, and levels of legitimacy (Deephouse & Suchman, 2008). Recently, Suddaby, Bitektine, and Haack (2017) have provided a thorough assessment of legitimacy, the different ways it has been defined, and where and how it occurs. Legitimacy is often included as one of the most important and impactful social evaluations, particularly in institutional research, where legitimacy drives organizational actions.

As stigma research has evolved, stigma has been shown to be its own distinct concept, unique from moral illegitimacy, although there is still some debate about this difference (see our dialogue with other stigma researchers about this topic in the *Journal of Management Inquiry*, Volume 28, Issue 1). While we agree and recognize the importance of legitimacy as a social evaluation and concept in much of organizational theory, we argue that it is distinctly different from stigma for several reasons. First, we argue that legitimacy is essentially a dichotomous categorization of an organization's appropriateness. Unlike stigma, which has different thresholds, antecedents, outcomes, and impacts, when it comes to legitimacy, organizations either are legitimate or not, illegitimate or not. Second, stigma is enacted through ostracizing the stigmatized. Depending on different dimensions of the audience, including size, power, and closeness, the stigma can be far-reaching or fairly innocuous. Finally, legitimacy and stigma operate in distinct dimensions that need to be studied separately; an organization can be stigmatized but legitimate. For instance, homeless shelters, despite their vital role in providing essential services, frequently encounter stigma. These shelters serve as legitimate institutions assisting vulnerable individuals, yet misconceptions and biases related to homelessness can lead to stigma.

4.2 Reputation

Reputation is the perception of the organization by key external stakeholders in particular and other outsiders more generally (Fombrun, 2001; Gioia & Thomas, 1996; Rao, 1994; Sutton & Callahan, 1987). Reputation is, by some measures, the most researched social evaluation in the management literature (George et al., 2016). In general, the work on reputation focuses on the perceptions of important stakeholders about the ability of an organization to functionally and pragmatically deliver the goods and services it promises and in general behave in ways that are expected as a good corporate or organizational citizen, such as providing consistent quality of products and appropriate levels of pay and benefits for their employees and not engaging in pollution or fraud. Many researchers have examined the role of reputation focusing on its positive effects, such as improved access to resources and increased opportunities for financial prosperity (Fombrun & Shanley, 1990; Rhee & Haunschild, 2006).

Devers et al. (2009) provided several good assessments of the differences between stigma and reputation. The key difference that Devers et al. (2009)

noted is that reputation individuates or differentiates the firm from its competitors, whereas stigma de-individuates organizations by giving them a general classification as stigmatized. Pollock et al. (2019) argued that reputation is primarily based on rational evaluative criteria while stigma is based principally on emotional and moral bases. Mishina and Devers (2012) also argued that equating stigma to bad reputation can "blur important boundaries, thereby limiting effective discussion, measurement, and estimation of these similar, but theoretically distinct, social evaluation constructs" (Mishina & Devers, 2012). For example, an organization may enjoy a positive pragmatic reputation with some social audiences, yet the organization may still be stigmatized by other key social audiences. An abortion service provider can be seen as effective and have high reputation in providing its service for its clients but other audiences – those opposing abortions – may still discredit it as a whole due to the service it provides (Hudson, 2008).

4.3 Status

Status is a complex and multilevel concept that affects individuals, organizations, and communities but broadly reflects the prestige granted an actor or organization because of its position in a social hierarchy (Piazza & Castellucci, 2014; Podolny, 1993). Status is therefore a method of enforcing social inequality, arguably unrelated to performance (Sauder, Lynn, & Podolny, 2012), that is based largely upon the relationship of one actor to other actors. Having high status has several advantages, including the ability to charge higher prices than competitors for similar quality goods (Benjamin & Podolny, 1999), attain lower costs from suppliers (Podolny, 1993), receive greater consideration in tournaments or other evaluations (Jensen, 2006; Washington & Zajac, 2005), access higher status trading partners (Castellucci & Ertug, 2010; Cowen, 2012), and numerous other benefits (Piazza & Castellucci, 2014). Although there has been a surge of research on status in recent years, the negative consequences of status have not been as widely explored (Kovács & Sharkey, 2014). While status may constrain the behavior of organizations, most notably by defining the set of interactions available to them (Sauder et al., 2012), most researchers agree that high status has overwhelmingly positive effects. As status is situated within the relationship with others, low status emphasizes more on organization's position within social hierarchy while stigma interests in whether an organization has a deep-seated flaw in the eyes of a group audiences. They are clearly two different concepts that it would be interesting to explore the relationship between stigma and status (see Section 5).

4.4 Celebrity

Organizational celebrity represents positive attention from audiences, resulting in their increasing willingness to exchange with the organization (Rindova et al., 2005; Zavyalova, Pfarrer, & Reger, 2017). Different from organizational reputation, the main socio-cognitive basis of celebrity rests on audiences' positive emotional responses toward the organization, rather than analytical and deliberate judgments (Pollock et al., 2019). Thus, organizational celebrity is similar to stigma in its evaluative dimensions with a highlight on emotional and moral factors (Pollock et al., 2019). Both processes are grounded in social sensemaking that draws on collective emotional responses instead of purely logical assessments or measurements (Wiesenfeld et al., 2008). Audiences attend to both the positive and negative actions of organization celebrities but often interpret events or behaviors that are tied to celebrities positively, and celebrities are often associated with positive, rather than negative, emotional responses (Zavyalova et al., 2017). Unlike stigma, scandals tied to celebrities are often forgiven, rather that exacerbated. While negative events can be attended to positively when celebrities are involved, stigmatized organizations are likely to receive further sanctions, not forgiveness.

Often the forgiveness bestowed upon celebrities is associated with impression management, as in the case of Starbucks, where an employee in Philadelphia called the police when two African-American men refused to leave. The store's CEO quickly apologized and instituted training across 8,000 Starbucks cafes. According to the CEO, sales were not affected (http://investor.Starbucks.com). As another example, despite selling personal data to Cambridge Analytica, a company which used the data to allegedly influence the 2016 US presidential election, Facebook's usership has continued to grow, arguably due to significant impression management tactics by its celebrity CEO, Mark Zuckerberg. Celebrities may have to engage in activities that exhibit a recognition of wrongdoing and a redirection of policy, but once repentance is communicated, celebrities are more likely to be forgiven by stakeholders (Thomas & Fowler, 2016). The compassion afforded to celebrities rests on a very different dimension than the discrimination bestowed upon the stigmatized. The role of impression management, however, is an important consideration in the stigmatization process as well.

4.5 Social Disapproval

Social disapproval has been used in several studies as a general term to describe negative social evaluation at an organizational level (Vergne, 2012; Zavyalova et al., 2012). Vergne (2012) defined social disapproval as the negative social evaluations of firms brought to public attention and measured it by views expressed by experts in newspapers. A specific definition of the term was recently offered by Wang et al. (2021a), referring to social disapproval as general enmity toward an organization from constituents, including both actively engaged ones such as stakeholders and passive observers (Wang et al., 2021b). Unlike Vergne (2012), Wang and colleagues defined social disapproval as a more automatic and intuitive reaction from constituents that often rely on "cognitive shorthand" (Mishina, Block, & Mannor, 2012: 460), which then can also trigger deliberative and analytical information processing (Bundy & Pfarrer, 2015). Unlike stigma that taints an organization due to deep-seated flaws and is hard to remove once established (Devers et al., 2009), social disapproval, based on the definition provided by Wang and colleagues (2021b), seems to capture a more general and intuitive negative reaction toward an organization.

Current research is limited on how stigma and social disapproval are related but clear differences exist. Similar to the visceral repugnance of dirty work, stigma is an extreme reaction whereas social disapproval has been viewed as anything from an intuitive and innocuous "feeling" to an outcomes-based measurement (Bundy & Pfarrer, 2015; Titus, Parker, & Bass, 2018). Examples of social disapproval can range from the waning popularity of religion in modern society to the general negative feelings associated with drilling companies that support fossil fuel production.

Organizational stigma is thus its own concept. Now that we have identified the social evaluations most commonly confused or associated with stigma, we next turn to future research directions.

5 Future Research

Despite the increasing scholarly attention to understanding and theorizing organizational stigma, to unleash its full potential as a theoretical lens to explore a distinct set of phenomena, more work is needed. In this section, we discuss some potential future research directions.

5.1 Definitional Clarity

5.1.1 Stigma, Stigmatization, and Experienced Stigma

Scholars of organizational stigma understand stigma as an outcome and stigmatization as a process; however, in empirical settings, it often quickly becomes muddled. So far, scholars have not yet specifically distinguished the related concepts of organizational stigma, organizational stigmatization, and experienced stigma of an organization. These concepts are also sometimes used interchangeably. Clarifying the concepts is crucial. First, it would clarify the key assumptions, scope, and boundary conditions related to these concepts and thus the phenomena they capture and explain. Second, addressing the differences between these concepts would help resolve the common challenges of organizational stigma scholars – how to demonstrate stigma/stigmatization/experienced stigma in empirical settings and how to operationalize and test them. Third, it would also facilitate knowledge accumulation, communication, and dissemination in the field of organizational stigma.

As we discuss in Section 3, organizational stigma refers to a socially constructed perception or evaluation of an organization by certain audiences as having a "deep-seated flaw" (Devers et al., 2009: 157; Goffman, 1963; Hudson, 2008; Sutton & Callahan, 1987). Stigmatization, on the other hand, is the social process of enacting and manifesting this negative social evaluation (Pescosolido & Martin, 2015), conducted by stigmatizers with the aim of nudging organizations into preferred or socially acceptable patterns of behavior. Experienced stigma of an organization, similar to felt stigma at the individual level, is an internal experience of how organizations perceive, interpret, suffer, and perhaps integrate this perception into their daily operations. Future research could use empirical studies to specify and distinguish the key features and attributes of these three concepts.

1. Future research could use a longitudinal study of an organization and its stigma, demonstrating empirical evidence of the process of stigmatization in the emergence phase, the establishment of stigma, stigmatization activities conducted after the stigma establishment, and how the organization interprets its own stigma, is impacted by it, and responds to it.
2. Future research could also use comparative case studies to explore under what conditions stigmatization activities lead to the establishment of organizational stigma and experienced stigma of an organization. These efforts could help clarify the relationships among these key constructs.
3. Future research could also develop better theorization on these concepts and develop a comprehensive theoretical framework.

Clarifying the differences between stigma, stigmatization, and experienced stigma could also inspire new research questions. For example:

4. How do organizations respond to stigmatization activities to successfully avoid and prevent the establishment of organizational stigma?
5. When does event stigma become internalized and experienced by an organization and turn into a source of organizational identity threat?

5.1.2 The Sources of Stigma

One area that has been understudied, despite previous calls for research, is the sources of stigma (Link & Phelan, 2001). An important condition of organizational stigma emergence is that an organization possesses a discrediting label that taints it as a whole. Such a discrediting label is often institutionalized and embedded in social structure, which reflects the fault lines in a society at any one point (Pescosolido & Martin, 2015). Current studies mostly focus on empirical contexts where an organization's disruptive behavior leads to the labeling processes, which then establish organizational stigma or explore organizations that operate in a category that is directly linked with a discrediting label. However, a more nuanced understanding of this process is needed:

1. How many violations/events are required for it to lead to the establishment of organizational stigma?
2. In the case of event stigma, what are the features and characteristics of the event and the organizations that facilitate the emergence of organizational stigma? How do these features and characteristics impact the emergence processes?
3. Are certain types of audiences more likely to assign organizational stigma?

Future research should also investigate changes in the macro-environment that might influence the interpretation of organizational behavior as an antecedent of stigma emergence. This is becoming an increasingly important area to explore. A growing number of studies show that key stakeholders target and stigmatize organizations not only for their disruptive activities but also for their inaction or lack of progress toward social and environmental problems such as global warming, gender inequality, data protection issues, and anti-abortion legislation.

4. When and how might an organization become targeted and carry stigma due to the change in the external environment? How do organizations respond to such changes to avoid stigma emergence?
5. How might a change in the macro-environment that reduces certain stigma facilitate the emergence of new forms of organizations?
6. How does the emergence of organizational stigma affect social movements?

The sources of stigma extend beyond the attributes or behaviors that may tarnish an organization as a whole; they can also stem from the locations of the organizations. Yet, much like organizations within stigmatized industries, the impact of such location-oriented stigma can vary. It depends on factors such as the centrality of location to organizations' operations and the feasibility of relocating. For example, Cowden et al. (2022) investigated how and why organizations can embrace location-oriented stigma by studying organizations in Detroit, a city that has long been associated with labels such as "most dangerous city" in the United States. Population and environmental health researchers have studied how place can impact stigmatization of certain groups and the assignment of stigma by certain audiences (Halliday, Brennan, Bambra, & Popay, 2021). Also, using a geopolitics perspective, Tsui-Auch et al. (2022) explored how interplays of stigma originating from different sources, including political ties with home-country government, impact audiences' reactions and organizations' response strategies. However, we still have a very limited understanding of how stigma stemming from locations impacts organizations and how organizations can manage it.

7. When and how does location-oriented stigma impact organizations operating within these locations?
8. How do organizations manage location-oriented stigma if relocating is not feasible?
9. Is it possible for organizations operating in stigmatized locations to destigmatize not only themselves but the location as well?

Finally, with regard to the sources of stigma, the role of power has been notably underspecified. Power is an important delineating factor impacting the differences between individual and organizational stigma. Individuals often lack the power to diminish their individual stigma, even though they are parts of groups, because such groups are often disparate or unorganized and membership is based on stigmatizing factors that the individuals may or may not embrace. Tyler and colleagues (Tyler & Slater, 2018; Tyler, 2018; Parker & Aggleton, 2003) have recognized that power is an understudied element of stigma research and that reinforcing beneficial inequalities is one of the underlying motivations for the reproduction of stigma. Notably, some of the foundational writings on stigma (namely Durkheim and Goffman) largely ignore the role that power has in reproducing social inequalities and injustice (Tyler, 2018). Building on questions that others have asked, we believe exploring the role of power in organizational stigma could be insightful:

10. How is power enacted by stigmatizing groups, both within and outside of organizations?
11. How does power reinforce or reconstruct social inequalities related to stigma among organizations within industries?
12. Do power differentials impact the methods stigmatizing groups utilize in organizational stigma? Particularly, when stigmatizing groups lack power, how do they engage in the stigmatization process and what are the outcomes?

5.1.3 The Effects of Stigma

As can be seen from examples of organizations that hide, use, or lose stigma in Section 3, most empirical studies of organizational stigma have focused on processes of stigma management rather than on the effects of stigmatization itself. The lack of a comprehensive understanding of the effects of stigma prevents us from understanding the full dynamics of stigma development and its effects and from exploring what exactly the organization is trying to prevent from happening. Future research could look into:

1. What are the effects of stigma and/or stigmatization on the target organization, its similar peers, its network partners, and its employees?
2. If the target organization failed to manage its stigma and/or stigmatization, what are the effects on the organization? Is it possible for this organization to fix the situation?
3. What role might positive social evaluation play in cases of event stigma? Does status or high reputation protect an organization even in cases of stigma?

5.1.4 Beyond Stigma Emergence

Stigmatization is the social process of enacting and manifesting the negative social evaluation (Pescosolido & Martin, 2015), as well as a purposive effort to contribute to a stigma's persistence. While previous work has highlighted the labeling and attribution processes of stigmatization in the phase of stigma emergence (Devers et al., 2009; Kitsuse, 1962; Wiesenfeld et al., 2008), less has been done to understand the stigmatization processes and practices beyond stigma emergence. Future research could look into events that might trigger active stigmatization and explore its processes and dynamics.

1. What are the events that might lead to active stigmatization after stigma emergence?
2. What are the motivations of stigmatizers in these circumstances and how do they impact the stigmatization processes?

5.2 Stigma as a Cross-Level Phenomenon

Stigma is a cross-level phenomenon and can move from and to the organization level (Thomson & Grandy, 2018; Zhang et al., 2021). For example, stigma that is embedded at an industry/category level means that organizations belonging to this industry are also highly likely to carry organizational stigma, depending on whether audiences are aware of the organization's membership in this industry (e.g., men's bathhouses, the tobacco industry, the pornography industry). Organizational stigma might also negatively impact individuals belonging to the organization. If the source of stigma is embedded at the industry/category level, it would be interesting to explore:

1. Do all industry members carry the same degree of organizational stigma (e.g., all bathhouses in the United States are stigmatized, but more or less so depending on the environment. European men's bathhouses seem less stigmatized)? So, what are the key factors that impact the degree of stigma attached to a specific organization? And how would similar organizations be impacted if the stigma of one organization becomes salient and it becomes actively stigmatized by audiences?
2. When is organizational stigma an organization versus an industry phenomenon?
3. Is it possible for organizations within the same industry to work together and manage the shared stigma (e.g., how did companies in the oil and gas industries in the 1970s work together to respond to the energy crisis that tainted the whole industry)? How do industry-/field-level associations ameliorate stigma?

In contrast, if the source of stigma is embedded at an organizational level, it would be interesting to explore:

4. What are the spillover effects to the industry of this organizational stigma? How do other members of the industry avoid or minimize the effects of the spillovers?
5. If the target organization is actively stigmatized by key audiences, how does this shape the dynamics and processes of stigmatization experienced by its similar peers?
6. How does organizational stigma impact the individuals associated with the organization?

If the source of stigma is embedded at the individual level (e.g., disruptive behaviors conducted by individuals of an organization, which then develop into the stigma attached to a person), it would be interesting to explore:

7. When and how does individual-level stigma move up to the organization level and lead to stigmatization of the organization? Does this process lead to the establishment of organizational stigma?
8. What characteristics of the individual stigma make it more likely it will develop into organizational stigma?

9. How does an organization respond to the threat of stigma transfer from an individual to prevent or minimize the negative impacts on itself?

5.3 The Emotional Dimension of Stigma and Stigmatization

Despite its importance in understanding stigma, stigmatization, and experienced stigma, little has been said about the emotional dimension related to organizational stigma. The only exception is Hampel and Tracey (2017), who demonstrated how stigmatizers' fear for their social position motivates stigmatization activities targeting an organization. The inattention to the role of emotion perhaps stems from the use of a cognitive lens to study organizational stigma, highlighting stigma as a signifier of organizations possessing deeply discrediting features that violate institutionalized norms and expectations. Incorporating emotions into organizational stigma research could help us fully understand the nature of stigma as a social evaluation and the dynamics of stigmatization. For example, in the #MeToo Movement, the emotional reactions from key stigmatizing audiences targeting specific organizations and individuals played a significant role in the process of exerting social control. Future research could look into:

1. What role can a specific type of emotion such as anger and fear play in facilitating the stigmatization processes and establishment of organizational stigma? Does emotion accelerate/slow down this process at both individual and collective levels?
2. If stigmatizing audiences experience different types of emotion (e.g., anger vs fear), should organizations respond to stigmatization activities differently and how?

5.4 Heterogeneous Audiences

As stigma is a socially constructed perception held by audiences and stigmatization is carried out by audiences, it is essential to understand how an organization is impacted and should respond to audiences with disparate values, conflicting ideologies, and irreconcilable belief systems (Hudson, 2008). In other words, the same organizational behaviors can be perceived and interpreted differently based on the rational, emotional, and moral assessments of different groups of audiences (Pollock et al., 2019). What is critical to one group could be quite irrelevant in another group's evaluations of the organization (Lamin & Zaheer, 2012). Also, sometimes some stakeholder groups, even though they hold negative opinions toward these activities/inactions, may overlook or keep silent about them (Adut,

2005). Taking these complex relationships into consideration would help us better understand how stigma impacts organizational behaviors and outcomes.

Previous studies have paid limited attention to the heterogeneity of audiences, with few exceptions. Using the context of a kink-focused student organization, Coslor et al. (2020) highlighted the importance of gaining official support for emergent organizations and how these organizations then can work toward moral legitimation with some audiences to embrace the relevant stigma, as well as the importance of developing appropriate discourse to gain such support. Wang et al. (2021) highlighted how different types of stakeholders, authoritative stakeholders, and primary stakeholders (i.e., the evaluators of and the groups who interact with professions on a daily basis) shape the stigmatization processes targeting a profession. Piazza and Augustine (2022) explored the survival of US abortion clinics in a context with polarized views on abortion and found that the absence of opposition to abortion (i.e., active stigmatization activities) is sufficient for survival in this industry or the support for abortion from state governors. Legislation can also enable clinics to survive despite challenges from the opposition.

The heterogeneity of audiences is becoming an increasingly interesting issue to look at. Due to the rise of social media in the last decades, audiences can easily disseminate their views (Piening et al., 2020; Wang et al., 2021b), making them salient among certain groups of audiences and even polarizing the views held by different groups of audiences. This amplifies the complexity of organizational stigma. Focusing on audiences and their perceptions facilitates a deeper understanding of how organizational stigma forms and evolves and how organizations can respond. Future research avenues could delve into:

1. How do organizations navigate relationships with disagreeing audiences (e.g., bathhouse customers vs. the "morality squad")?
2. When key groups of audiences hold different views (e.g., on abortion), what do the stigmatization dynamics look like? When does stigma escalate, and when does it diminish? Does this process lead to unexpected outcomes? How do organizations weigh these different evaluations?
3. How can different audiences be meaningfully categorized considering their power, social influence, and relationships with the stigmatized target that drive the different, even polarized, evaluations?

5.5 Stigma and Other Social Evaluations

Stigma and related social evaluations have received significant attention in recent years. As we discuss in Section 4, many social evaluations have largely positive outcomes for the organizations or individuals involved; however, stigma is overwhelmingly negative. As different social evaluations provide different lenses to understand an organization (reputation on performance, status on a firm's position in social hierarchy, etc.) and they can exist and impact organizations simultaneously, it would be interesting to explore and compare social evaluations in empirical settings. For example, the complexity of the relationship between status and stigma is contingent on contextual and circumstantial factors, whereby high status may protect against stigma in some instances, while exacerbating it in others. Future research could investigate:

1. When firms operate in a stigmatized industry, does a high reputation lead to similar positive outcomes as in non-stigmatized industries?
2. What does a firm's status look like when it operates in a stigmatized industry? Do audiences interpret the high status differently?
3. How do the reputation and status of an organization impact the outcome of stigmatization?
4. Does impression management backfire when an organization operates in a stigmatized industry and when an organization suffers from event stigma?
5. What are the relationships between stigma, scandal, and misconduct?

5.6 Stigma and Stigmatization as a Double-Edged Sword

Stigma is often defined as a discrediting attribute. Previous studies have mainly focused on the negative side of stigma, either by theorizing the negative outcomes associated with stigma or by demonstrating the ways to manage stigma and prevent or minimize the negative outcomes. However, as discussed earlier, given that stigma is socially constructed and a perception held by audiences, this negativity is not fixed and can be interpreted differently due to the evolution of the macro-environment and the heterogeneity of the audience. Thus, stigma is not absolute and can have different meanings across situations, cultures, and times (Ashforth & Kreiner, 2014; Jones & King, 2014), which can have both positive and negative implications. For example, Helms and Patterson (2014) highlighted that MMA organizations used stigma to their advantage by drawing some supportive audiences' attention. Tracey and Phillips (2016) also demonstrated a set of positive outcomes of stigmatization, showing how stigmatization toward a social service agency caused by serving migrants eventually increased the organization's profile as the discrediting attribute it held represented values that other audiences uphold and promote. However, this topic is still undertheorized. Future research could look into:

1. Under what conditions does stigma lead to positive outcomes? And for whom?

2. For core-stigmatized organizations, under what conditions does stigma become a source of identity or pride?

5.7 Stigma Research as a Tool to Understand Social Issues

Scholars have recognized that "stigma can be a call to action to overcome discrimination and restore justice" (Paetzold, Dipboye, & Elsbach, 2008: 191). For example, it can be utilized as a form of entrepreneurial emancipation (Coslor et al., 2020; Ruebottom & Toubiana, 2021). It can encourage resilience and posttraumatic growth (Staub & Vollhardt, 2008). When groups are stigmatized, organizations may organize, either formally or informally, as a way of either providing support to members of the group or collectively resisting stigma (Savio, 2017; Wang & Tracey, forthcoming). These organizations can have strong cultural elements and evoke emotional commitment, opposition, or identification from stakeholders. Developing a holistic understanding of stigmatization dynamics and stigma in these empirical contexts would help us understand how to address the barriers to building an inclusive society. Future research could look into:

1. How do organizations serving marginalized groups help address the stigmatization and exclusion experienced by these groups?
2. How do organizations serving marginalized groups facilitate a sense of pride among their employees and support marginalized groups to cope with their internalized stigmatization?
3. How do organizations serving marginalized groups utilize their stigma to draw attention to focal issues in society and help reconstruct the meanings attached to these issues?

5.8 Methodological Innovations

As highlighted in our discussion on methodologies, much of stigma research has been longitudinal with qualitative components. This is imperative, considering the multiplicity of audiences involved and the necessity of elucidating the context and situations of stigmatized firms. This necessity also serves as a barrier to advancing knowledge in the area, however. As Grandy, Mavin, and Simpson (2014) have stated, academic research is often biased toward large data sets and quantitative methods; therefore, the necessity of rich, qualitative data can deter some less innovative outlets from publishing research in the area. Still, the acquisition of rich data serves as a cornerstone, enabling researchers to develop a nuanced understanding of the context and present convincing evidence to audiences that organizational stigma or related phenomena such as stigmatization or experienced stigma exist. Researchers have found ways to support such research by presenting mixed-methods approaches, such as using fuzzy-set qualitative comparative analysis (fsQCA) along with qualitative analysis (Augustine & Piazza, 2022) or by employing artificial intelligence programs to search within (not interpret) large qualitative data sets for stigma-related phenomenon. Some work in this area has already begun (e.g., see the work of Schildt and others on digital strategy), and researchers employing new methodologies or software should encourage innovation without sacrificing the rigor necessary for accurate interpretation.

Another important innovation in stigma research concerns the use of multimedia data sources. The development of technology with which both organizations and audiences can express, share, and disseminate their values, emotions, and norms in various forms, including, but not limited to, text, image, and video means that scholars have access to an increasing number of sources for analysis. For example, Werner, Punzi, and Turkenburg (2024) used visual data as a part of their secondary data to document social entrepreneurs' efforts to combat the stigma associated with menstruation. To develop a more holistic understanding of empirical contexts and to potentially broaden the scope beyond what traditional data collection tools may capture, stigma scholars should embrace innovative methodologies. These methods are essential for effectively encapsulating stigma and its associated dynamics, ensuring a comprehensive exploration of these complex phenomena.

1. How can we acknowledge and encourage technological and methodological innovations in empirical analysis without sacrificing the rigor necessary for the nuanced understanding required to research stigma?
2. How can we use methods from other disciplines such as international management to inform our understanding of cross-cultural comparisons of stigma?

6 Conclusion

Organizational stigma has moved from being a phenomenon left to the fields of criminology, social psychology, healthcare, and sociology to mainstream business research. Once seen as a social issue with minimal economic impact, management scholars have come to recognize the relevance of stigmatized organizations in managing everything from organizational culture to capital expenditures. Although certain industries and professions may be stigmatized across numerous places and audiences, stigma pervades each organization to some extent. Since evaluation is a socio-cognitive process, organizations should be aware of the effects of stigma and its impacts on a myriad of organizational factors. As identified, there are still many areas that merit further investigation within organizational stigma. Doubtless more will emerge with time and the changing societal, technical, and global landscape. Our purpose in writing this Element is to offer a summary of what has been done and provide some clear paths forward based on the current state of research to help us understand the important role that stigma and other social evaluations play in business and their important role in society.

References

Adut, A. (2005). A theory of scandal: Victorians, homosexuality, and the fall of Oscar Wilde. *American Journal of Sociology, 111*(1), 213–248.

Aldrich, H. E., & Fiol, C. M. (1994). Fools rush in? The institutional context of industry creation. *Academy of Management Review, 19*(4), 645–670.

Anteby, M. (2010). Markets, morals, and practices of trade: Jurisdictional disputes in the U.S. Commerce in cadavers. *Administrative Science Quarterly, 55*(4), 606–638.

Anteby, M., & Anderson, C. (2014). The shifting landscape of LGBT organizational research. *Research in Organizational Behavior, 34*, 3–25.

Ashforth, B. E. (2019). Stigma and legitimacy: Two ends of a single continuum or different continua altogether? *Journal of Management Inquiry, 28*(1), 22–30.

Ashforth, B. E., & Kreiner, G. E. (1999). "How can you do it?": Dirty work and the challenge of constructing a positive identity. *Academy of Management Review, 24*(3), 413–434.

Ashforth, B. E., & Kreiner, G. E. (2014). Dirty work and dirtier work: Differences in countering physical, social, and moral stigma. *Management and Organization Review, 10*(1), 81–108.

Ashforth, B. E., Kreiner, G. E., Clark, M. A., & Fugate, M. (2007). Normalizing dirty work: Managerial tactics for countering occupational taint. *Academy of Management Journal, 50*(1), 149–174.

Barlow, M. A., Verhaal, J. C., & Hoskins, J. D. (2018). Guilty by association: Product-level category stigma and audience expectations in the U.S. Craft beer industry. *Journal of Management, 44*(7), 2934–2960.

Benjamin, B. A., & Podolny, J. M. (1999). Status, quality, and social order in the California wine industry. *Administrative Science Quarterly, 44*(3), 563–589.

Benner, M. J., & Ranganathan, R. A. M. (2012). Offsetting illegitimacy? How pressures from securities analysts influence incumbents in the face of new technologies. *Academy of Management Journal, 55*(1), 213–233.

Bitektine, A. (2011). Toward a theory of social judgments of organizations: The case of legitimacy, reputation, and status. *Academy of Management Review, 36*(1), 151–179.

Blumer, H. 1969. *Symbolic interactionism: Perspective and method.* Englewood Cliffs, NJ: Prentice-Hall.

Brulliard, K. (2003). Abortion clinics targeted before they are built; foes threaten to boycott contractors. *The Washington Post*, November 30, Sunday, p. A01.

Bundy, J., & Pfarrer, M. D. (2015). A burden of responsibility: The role of social approval at the onset of a crisis. *Academy of Management Review*, *40*(3), 345–369.

Campana, M., Duffy, K., & Micheli, M. R. (2022). "We're all born naked and the rest is drag": Spectacularization of core stigma in Rupaul's drag race. *Journal of Management Studies*, *59*(8), 1950–1986.

Carberry, E. J., & King, B. G. (2012). Defensive practice adoption in the face of organizational stigma: Impression management and the diffusion of stock option expensing. *Journal of Management Studies*, *49*(7), 1137–1167.

Castellucci, F., & Ertug, G. (2010). What's in it for them? Advantages of higher-status partners in exchange relationships. *Academy of Management Journal*, *53*(1), 149–166.

Cavender, G., Gray, K., & Miller, K. W. (2010). Enron's perp walk: Status degradation ceremonies as narrative. *Crime, Media, Culture*, *6*(3), 251–266.

Chaudoir, S. R., Earnshaw, V. A., & Andel, S. (2013). "Discredited" versus "discreditable": Understanding how shared and unique stigma mechanisms affect psychological and physical health disparities. *Basic and Applied Social Psychology*, *35*(1), 75–87.

Clair, J. A., Beatty, J. E., & MacLean, T. L. (2005). Out of sight but not out of mind: Managing invisible social identities in the workplace. *Academy of Management Review*, *30*(1), 78–96.

Clemente, M., & Roulet, T. J. (2015). Public opinion as a source of deinstitutionalization: A "spiral of silence" approach. *Academy of Management Review*, *40*(1), 96–114.

Coslor, E. H., Crawford, B., & Brents, B. G. (2020). Whips, chains, and books on campus: How emergent organizations with core stigma gain official recognition. *Journal of Management Inquiry*, *29*(3), 299–316.

Cowden, B. J., Bendickson, J. S. Mathias, B. D., & Solomon, S. J. (2022). Straight OUTTA Detroit: Embracing stigma as part of the entrepreneurial narrative. *Journal of Management Studies*, *59*(8), 1915–1949.

Cowen, A. P. (2012). An expanded model of status dynamics: The effects of status transfer and interfirm coordination. *Academy of Management Journal*, *55*(5), 1169–1186.

Cowen, A. P., & Marcel, J. J. (2011). Damaged goods: Board decisions to dismiss reputationally compromised directors. *Academy of Management Journal*, *54*(3), 509–527.

Creed, W. E. D., DeJordy, R., & Lok, J. (2010). Being the change: Resolving institutional contradiction through identity work. *Academy of Management Journal*, *53*(6), 1336–1364.

References

Creed, W. E. D., Hudson, B. A., Okhuysen, G. A., & Smith-Crowe, K. (2014). Swimming in a sea of shame: Incorporating emotion into explanations of institutional reproduction and change. *Academy of Management Review, 39*(3), 275–301.

Cruz-Inigo, A. E., Ladizinski, B., & Sethi, A. (2011). Albinism in Africa: Stigma, slaughter and awareness campaigns. *Dermatologic Clinics, 29*(1), 79–87.

D'Aunno, T., Sutton, R. I., & Price, R. H. (1991). Isomorphism and external support in conflicting institutional environments: A study of drug abuse treatment units. *Academy of Management Journal, 34*(3), 636–661.

Davidson, D. K. (1996). *Selling sin: The marketing of socially unacceptable products*. Westport: Quorum Books.

Dean, D. H. (2010). Consumer perceptions of visible tattoos on service personnel. *Managing Service Quality: An International Journal, 20*(3), 294–308.

Dean, D. H. (2011). Young adult perception of visible tattoos on a white-collar service provider. *Young Consumers, 12*(3), 254–264.

Deephouse, D. L., & Suchman, M. (2008). Legitimacy in organizational institutionalism. In R. Greenwood, C. Oliver, K. Sahlin, & R. Suddaby (Eds.), *The Sage handbook of organizational institutionalism*, 49–77. London: Sage.

DeJordy, R. (2008). Just passing through: Stigma, passing, and identity decoupling in the work place. *Group & Organization Management, 33*(5), 504–531.

Desai, V. M. (2011). Mass media and massive failures: Determining organizational efforts to defend field legitimacy following crises. *Academy of Management Journal, 54*(2), 263–278.

Devers, C. E., Dewett, T., Mishina, Y., & Belsito, C. A. (2009). A general theory of organizational stigma. *Organization Science, 20*(1), 154–171.

Devers, C. E., & Mishina, Y. (2019). Comments on stigma versus legitimacy. *Journal of Management Inquiry, 28*(1), 16–21.

Dong, L., Hudson, B. A., Moura, D., & Jarvis, L. C. (2023). Amplifying stigmatization: Owlcatraz and the naming of a football stadium. *Organization Studies, 44*(7), 1055–1080.

Douglas, M. (1966). *Purity and danger: An analysis of concepts of pollution and taboo*. London: Routledge.

Durand, R., & Vergne, J.-P. (2015). Asset divestment as a response to media attacks in stigmatized industries. *Strategic Management Journal, 36*(8), 1205–1223.

Durkheim, É. (1895; 1982). *The rules of sociological method*. Paris: Alcan.

Durkheim, É. (1897; 1951). *Suicide: A study in sociology*. Paris: Alcan.

Dutton, J. E., & Dukerich, J. M. (1991). Keeping an eye on the mirror: Image and identity in organizational adaptation. *Academy of Management Journal, 34*(3), 517–554.

Elsbach, K. D., & Sutton, R. I. (1992). Acquiring organizational legitimacy through illegitimate actions: A marriage of institutional and impression management theories. *Academy of Management Journal, 35*(4), 699–738.

Fombrun, C. (1996). *Reputation, Harvard Business School Press*. Boston, MA: Harvard Business School Press.

Fombrun, C. J. (2001). Corporate reputation – Its measurement and management. *Thexis, 18*(4), 23–26.

Fombrun, C., & Shanley, M. (1990). What's in a name? Reputation building and corporate strategy. *Academy of Management Journal, 33*(2), 233–258.

Frandsen, S., & Morsing, M. (2022). Behind the stigma shield: Frontline employees' emotional response to organizational event stigma at work and at home. *Journal of Management Studies, 59*(8), 1987–2023.

Galvin, T. L., Ventresca, M. J., & Hudson, B. A. (2004). Contested industry dynamics. *International Studies of Management & Organization, 34*(4), 56–82.

Gardberg, N. A., & Newburry, W. (2013). Who boycotts whom? Marginalization, company knowledge, and strategic issues. *Business & Society, 52*(2), 318–357.

Gardberg, N. A., Newburry, W. Hudson, B. A., & Viktora-Jones, M. (2022). Adoption of LGBT-inclusive policies: Social construction, coercion, or competition?, *Social Forces, 101*(3), 1116–1142. https://doi.org/10.1093/sf/soac033.

George, G., Dahlander, L., Graffin, S. D., & Sim, S. (2016). Reputation and status: Expanding the role of social evaluations in management research. *Academy of Management Journal, 59*(1), 1–13.

Gilman, C. (1898). *Women and Economics: A study of the economic relation between men and women as a factor in social evolution*. Boston, MA: Small, Maynard.

Ginzel, L. E., Kramer, R. M., & Sutton, R. I. (1992). Organizational impression management as a reciprocal influence process: The neglected role of the organizational audience. *Research in Organizational Behavior, 15*, 227–267.

Gioia, D. A., & Thomas, J. B. (1996). Identity, image, and issue interpretation: Sensemaking during strategic change in academia. *Administrative Science Quarterly, 41*(3), 370–403. https://doi.org/10.2307/2393936

Glerum, D. R. (2021). Tainted heroes: The emergence of dirty work during pandemics. Industries and Organizational Psychology: *Perspectives on Science and Practice*, 14(1–2), 41–44.

Goffman, E. (1963). *Stigma: Notes on the management of spoiled identity*. Englewood, CO: Prentice-Hall.

Grandy, G., Mavin, S., & Simpson, R. (2014). Doing dirty research using qualitative methodologies: Lessons from stigmatized occupations. *Qualitative Research in Organizations and Management*, *9*(3). https://doi.org/10.1108/QROM-06-2014-1228.

Grattet, R. (2011). Societal reactions to deviance. *Annual Review of Sociology*, *37*(1), 185–204.

Greenwood, R., Oliver, C., Lawrence, T. B., & Meyer, R. E. (2017). *The SAGE handbook of organizational institutionalism*. London. SAGE, https://doi.org/10.4135/9781526415066.

Greve, H. R., Palmer, D., & Pozner, J.-E. (2010). Organizations gone wild: The causes, processes, and consequences of organizational misconduct. *The Academy of Management Annals*, *4*, 53–107.

Grougiou, V., Dedoulis, E., & Leventis, S. (2016). Corporate social responsibility reporting and organizational stigma: The case of "sin" industries. *Journal of Business Research*, *69*(2), 905–914.

Gulli, C., Kohler, N., & Patriquin, M. (2007). The great university cheating scandal. *Maclean's*, *120*(5), 32–36.

Gutierrez, B., Howard-Grenville, J., & Scully, M. A. (2010). The faithful rise up: Split identification and an unlikely change effort. *Academy of Management Journal*, *53*(4), 673–699.

Halliday, E. Brennan, L., Bambra, C., & Popay, J. (2020). The elephant in the room? Why spatial stigma does not receive the public health attention it deserves. *Journal of Public Health*, *42*(1), 38–43.

Halliday, E., Brennan, L., Bambra, C., & Popay, J. (2021). 'It is surprising how much nonsense you hear': How residents experience and react to living in a stigmatised place. A narrative synthesis of the qualitative evidence. *Health & Place*, *68*, 102525. https://doi.org/10.1016/j.healthplace.2021.102525.

Hamilton, P., Redman, T., & McMurray, R. (2019). "Lower than a snake's belly": Discursive constructions of dignity and heroism in low-status garbage work. *Journal of Business Ethics*, *156*(4), 889–901.

Hampel, C. E., & Tracey, P. (2017). How organizations move from stigma to legitimacy: The case of cook's travel agency in Victorian Britain. *Academy of Management Journal*, *60*(6), 2175–2207.

Harding, D. J., Fox, C., & Mehta, J. D. (2002). Studying rare events through qualitative case studies: Lessons from a study of rampage school shootings. *Sociological Methods & Research*, *31*, 174–217.

Helms, W. S., & Patterson, K. D. W. (2014). Eliciting acceptance for "illicit" organizations: The positive implications of stigma for MMA organizations. *Academy of Management Journal*, *57*(5), 1453–1484.

Helms, W. S., Patterson, K. D. W., & Hudson, B. A. (2019). Let's not "taint" stigma research with legitimacy, please. *Journal of Management Inquiry, 28* (1), 5–10.

Herek, G. M. (1998). *Stigma and sexual orientation: Understanding prejudice against lesbians, gay men, and bisexuals.* Thousand Oaks, CA: Sage.

Hernandez, B., McDonald, K., Divilbiss, M., et al. (2008). Reflections from employers on the disabled workforce: Focus groups with healthcare, hospitality and retail administrators. *Employee Responsibilities and Rights Journal, 20*(3), 157–164.

Hilgartner, S., & Bosk, C. L. (1988). The rise and fall of social problems: A public arenas model. *American Journal of Sociology, 94*(1), 53–78.

Hills, S., Voronov, M., & Hinings, C. B. (2013). Putting new wine in old bottles: Utilizing rhetorical history to overcome stigma associated with a previously dominant logic. *Research in the Sociology of Organizations, 39,* 99–137.

Hsu, G., & Grodal, S. (2021). The double-edged sword of oppositional category positioning: A study of the U.S. E-cigarette category, 2007–2017. *Administrative Science Quarterly, 66*(1), 86–132.

Hudson, B. A. (2008). Against all odds: A consideration of core-stigmatized organizations. *Academy of Management Review, 33*(1), 252–266.

Hudson, B. A., & Okhuysen, G. A. (2009). Not with a ten-foot pole: Core stigma, stigma transfer, and improbable persistence of men's bathhouses. *Organization Science, 20*(1), 134–153.

Hudson, B. A., & Okhuysen, G. A. (2014). Taboo topics: Structural barriers to the study of organizational stigma. *Journal of Management Inquiry, 23*(3), 242–253.

Hudson, B. A., Okhuysen, G. A., & Creed, W. E. D. (2015). Power and institutions: Stones in the road and some yellow bricks. *Journal of Management Inquiry, 24*(3), 233–238.

Hughes, E. C. (1984). Bastard institutions. In *The sociological eye: Selected papers.* New Brunswick, NJ: Transaction Books.

Jarvis, L. C., Goodrick, E., & Hudson, B. A. (2019). Where the heart functions best: Reactive–affective conflict and the disruptive work of animal rights organizations. *Academy of Management Journal, 62*(5), 1358–1387.

Jensen, M. (2006). Should we stay or should we go? Accountability, status anxiety, and client defections. *Administrative Science Quarterly, 51*(1), 97–128.

Jensen, M. (2010). Legitimizing illegitimacy: How creating market identity legitimizes illegitimate products. *Research in the Sociology of Organizations, 31,* 39–80.

Jensen, T., & Tyler, I. (2015). "Benefits broods": The cultural and political crafting of anti-welfare commonsense. *Critical Policy Studies, 35,* 470–491.

Jones, E. E., Farina, A., Hastorf, A. H., et al. (1984). *Social stigma: The psychology of marked relationships*. New York, NY: W. H. Freeman.

Jones, K. P., & King, E. B. (2014). Managing concealable stigmas at work: A review and multilevel model. *Journal of Management*, 40(5), 1466–1494.

Jonsson, S., Greve, H. R., & Fujiwara-Greve, T. (2009). Undeserved loss: The spread of legitimacy loss to innocent organizations in response to reported corporate deviance. *Administrative Science Quarterly*, 54(2), 195–228.

Kalichman, S. C. (2013). The harms of internalized aids stigma: A comment on Tsai et al. *Annals of Behavioral Medicine*, 46(3), 256–257.

Khessina, O. M., Reis, S., & Verhaal, J. C. (2021). Stepping out of the shadows: Identity exposure as a remedy for stigma transfer concerns in the medical marijuana market. *Administrative Science Quarterly*, 66(3), 569–611.

Kim, H., & Jensen, M. (2014). Audience heterogeneity and the effectiveness of market signals: How to overcome liabilities of foreignness in film exports? *Academy of Management Journal*, 57(5), 1360–1384.

Kipping, M., & Üsdiken, B. (2014). History in organization and management theory: More than meets the eye. *Academy of Management Annals*, 8(1), 535–588.

Kitsuse, J. I. (1962). Social reaction to deviance: Problems of theory and method. *Social Problems*, 9, 247–256.

Kovács, B., & Sharkey, A. J. (2014). The paradox of publicity: How awards can negatively affect the evaluation of quality. *Administrative Science Quarterly*, 59(1), 1–33.

Kreiner, G. E., Ashforth, B. E., & Sluss, D. M. (2006). Identity dynamics in occupational dirty work: Integrating social identity and system justification perspectives. *Organization Science*, 17(5), 619–636.

Kreiner, G. E., Mihelcic, C. A., & Mikolon, S. (2022). Stigmatized work and stigmatized workers. *Annual Review of Organizational Psychology and Organizational Behavior*, 9, 95–120.

Kristeva, J., & Herman, J. (2010). Liberty, equality, fraternity, and … Vulnerability. *Women's Studies Quarterly*, 38(1/2), 251–268.

Kulik, C. T., Bainbridge, H. T. J., & Cregan, C. (2008). Known by the company we keep: Stigma-by-association effects in the workplace. *Academy of Management Review*, 33(1), 216–230.

Lamin, A., & Zaheer, S. (2012). Wall street vs. Main street: Firm strategies for defending legitimacy and their impact on different stakeholders. *Organization Science*, 23(1), 47–66.

Lashley, K., & Pollock, T. G. (2020). Waiting to inhale: Reducing stigma in the medical cannabis industry. *Administrative Science Quarterly*, 65(2), 434–482.

Lauriano, L. A., & Coacci, T. (2023). Losing control: The uncertain management of concealable stigmas when work and social media Collide. *Academy of Management Journal*, *66*(1): 222–247.

Link, B. G., & Phelan, J. C. (2001). Conceptualizing stigma. *Annual Review of Sociology*, *27*, 363–385.

Lyons, B. J., Pek, S., & Wessel, J. L. (2017). Toward α "sunlit path": Stigma identity management as α source of localized social change through interaction. *Academy of Management Review*, *42*(4), 618–636.

MacLean, T., & Behnam, M. (2010). Organizations: The dangers of decoupling: The relationship between compliance programs, legitimacy perceptions, and institutionalized misconduct. *Academy of Management Journal*, *53*(6), 1499–1520, available at SSRN: https://ssrn.com/abstract=2019165.

Magee, J. C., & Galinsky, A. D. (2008). 8 social hierarchy: The self-reinforcing nature of power and status. *Academy of Management Annals*, *2*(1), 351–398.

Marcel, J. J., & Cowen, A. P. (2014). Cleaning house or jumping ship? Understanding board upheaval following financial fraud. *Strategic Management Journal*, *35*(6), 926–937.

Melton, E. N., & MacCharles, J. D. (2021). Examining sport marketing through a rainbow lens. *Sport Management Review*, *24*(3), 421–438. https://doi.org/10.1080/14413523.2021.1880742.

Merton, R. K. (1968). *Social theory and social structure*. New York, NY: Simon and Schuster.

Mikolon, S., Kreiner, G. E., & Wieseke, J. (2016). Seeing you seeing me: Stereotypes and the stigma magnification effect. *Journal of Applied Psychology*, *101*(5), 639–656.

Mishina, Y., Block, E. S., & Mannor, M. J. (2012). The path dependence of organizational reputation: How social judgment influences assessments of capability and character. *Strategic Management Journal*, *33*(5), 459–477.

Mishina, Y., & Devers, C. E. (2012). On being bad: Why stigma is not the same as a bad reputation. In T. G. Pollock & M. L. Barnett (Eds.), *The Oxford Handbook of Corporate Reputation*, (online edn), Oxford Academic, https://doi.org/10.1093/oxfordhb/9780199596706.013.0010.

Moore, C., Stuart, H. C., & Pozner, J.-E. (2010). Avoiding the consequences of repeated misconduct: Stigma's licence and stigma's transferability. UC Berkeley: Institute for Research on Labor and Employment. Retrieved from https://escholarship.org/uc/item/1q97p1bs.

Narendran, R., Reveley, J., & Almeida, S. (2021). Coutnering transphobic stigma: Identity work by self-employed Keralan transpeople. *Gender, Work & Organization*, *28*(4), 1220–1236.

Negro, G., Williams, M. J., Pontikes, E. G., & Lopiano, G. (2021). Destigmatization and its imbalanced effects in labor markets. *Management Science, 67*(12), 7669–7686. https://doi.org/10.1287/mnsc.2020.3881.

Paetzold, R. L., Dipboye, R. L., & Elsbach, K. D. (2008). A new look at stigmatization in and of organizations. *Academy of Management Review, 33*(1), 186–193.

Parker, R., & Aggleton, P. (2003). HIV and AIDS-related stigma and discrimination: A conceptual framework and implications for action. *Social Sciences & Medicine, 57*(1), 13–24. doi: 10.1016/s0277-9536(02)00304-0. PMID: 12753813.

Paruchuri, S., & Misangyi, V. F. (2015). Investor perceptions of financial misconduct: The heterogeneous contamination of bystander firms. *Academy of Management Journal, 58*(1), 169–194.

Patock-Peckham, J. A., Canning, J. R., & Leeman, R. F. (2018). Shame is bad and guilt is good: An examination of the impaired control over drinking pathway to alcohol use and related problems. *Personality and Individual Differences, 121*, 62–66.

Patriotta, G., Gond, J.-P., & Schultz, F. (2011). Maintaining legitimacy: Controversies, orders of worth, and public justifications. *Journal of Management Studies, 48*(8), 1804–1836.

Patterson, K. D. W., Hudson, B. A., & Helms, W. S. (2019). Introduction: A dialog on stigma versus legitimacy, and how they relate to organizations and their actors. *Journal of Management Inquiry, 28*(1), 3–4.

Pescosolido, B. A., & Martin, J. K. (2015). The stigma complex. *Annual Review of Sociology, 41*(1), 87–116.

Pfarrer, M. D., Decelles, K. A., Smith, K. G., & Taylor, M. S. (2008). After the fall: Reintegrating the corrupt organization. *Academy of Management Review, 33*(3), 730–749.

Phelan, J. C., Bromet, E. J., & Link, B. G. (1998). Psychiatric illness and family stigma. *Schizophrenia Bulletin, 24*(1), 115–126.

Phillips, D. J., Turco, C. J., & Zuckerman, E. W. (2013). Betrayal as market barrier: Identity-based limits to diversification among high-status corporate law firms. *American Journal of Sociology, 118*(4), 1023–1054.

Phung, K., Buchanan, S., Toubiana, M., Ruebottom, T., & Turchick-Hakak, L. (2021). When stigma doesn't transfer: Stigma deflection and occupational stratification in the sharing economy. *Journal of Management Studies, 58*(4), 1107–1139.

Piazza, A., & Augustine, G. L. (2022). Nevertheless, they persisted: How patterns of opposition and support shaped the survival of U.S. Abortion clinics. *Journal of Management Studies, 59*(8), 2124–2153.

Piazza, A., & Castellucci, F. (2014). Status in organization and management theory. *Journal of Management*, *40*(1), 287–315.

Piazza, A., & Jourdan, J. (2017). When the dust settles: The consequences of scandals for organizational competition. *Academy of Management Journal*, 61(1), 165–190.

Piazza, A., & Perretti, F. (2015). Categorical stigma and firm disengagement: Nuclear power generation in the united states, 1970–2000. *Organization Science*, *26*(3), 724–742.

Piening, E. P., Salge, T. O., Antons, D., & Kreiner, G. E. (2020). Standing together or falling apart? Understanding employees' responses to organizational identity threats. *Academy of Management Review*, *45*(2), 325–351.

Podolny, J. M. (1993). A status-based model of market competition. *American Journal of Sociology*, *98*(4), 829–872.

Pollock, T. G., Lashley, K., Rindova, V. P., & Han, J.-H. (2019). Which of these things are not like the others? Comparing the rational, emotional, and moral aspects of reputation, status, celebrity, and stigma. *Academy of Management Annals*, *13*(2), 444–478.

Pontikes, E., Negro, G., & Rao, H. (2010). Stained red: A study of stigma by association to blacklisted artists during the "red scare" in Hollywood, 1945 to 1960. *American Sociological Review*, *75*(3), 456–478.

Pozner, J.-E. (2008). Stigma and settling up: An integrated approach to the consequences of organizational misconduct for organizational elites. *Journal of Business Ethics*, *80*(1), 141–150.

Pryor, J. B., Reeder, G. D., Yeadon, C., & Hesson-McInnis, M. (2004). A dual-process model of reactions to perceived stigma. *Journal of Personality and Social Psychology*, *87*(4), 436–452.

Ragin, B. R. (2008). Disclosure disconnects: Antecedents and consequences of disclosing invisible stigmas across life domains. *Academy of Management Review*, 33(1), 194–215.

Rao, H. (1994). The social construction of reputation: Certification contests, legitimation, and the survival of organizations in the American Automobile Industry: 1895–1912. *Strategic Management Journal*, *15*(51), 29–44.

Rhee, M., & Haunschild, P. R. (2006). The liability of good reputation: A study of product recalls in the U.S. Automobile industry. *Organization Science, 17*(1), 101–117.

Rindova, V. P., Pollock, T. G., & Hayward, M. L. (2006). Celebrity firms: The social construction of market popularity. *Academy of Management Review*, *31*(1), 50–71.

Rindova, V. P., Williamson, I. O., Petkova, A. P., & Sever, J. M. (2005). Being good or being known: An empirical examination of the dimensions, antecedents, and consequences of organizational reputation. *Academy of Management Journal, 48*(6), 1033–1049.

Roulet, T. (2015). "What good is wall street?" institutional contradiction and the diffusion of the stigma over the finance industry. *Journal of Business Ethics, 130*(2), 389–402.

Roulet, T. J. (2020). *The power of being divisive: Understanding negative social evaluations*. Redwood City, CA: Stanford University Press.

Ruebottom, T., & Toubiana, M. (2017). Biographical opportunities: How entrepreneurship creates pride in alterity in stigmatized fields. *Academy of Management Proceedings, 2017*(1), https://doi.org/10.5465/AMBPP.2017.12168abstract.

Ruebottom, T., & Toubiana, M. (2021). Constraints and opportunities of stigma: Entrepreneurial emancipation in the sex industry. *Academy of Management Journal, 64*(4), 1049–1077.

Ruebottom, T., Buchanan, S., Voronov, M., & Toubiana, M. (2022). Commercializing the practice of voyeurism: How organizations leverage authenticity and transgression to create value. *Academy of Management Review*, 47(3), 466–488.

Sauder, M., Lynn, F., & Podolny, J. M. (2012). Status: Insights from organizational sociology. *Annual Review of Sociology, 38*(1), 267–283.

Savio, G. (2017). Organization and stigma management: A comparative study of dumpster divers in New York. *Sociological Perspectives, 60*(2), 416–430.

Shantz, S., Fischer, A., Liu, E., & Levesque, A. (2019). Spoils from the Spoiled: Strategies for Entering Stigmatized Markets. *Journal of Management Studies*, 56, 1260–1286.

Simonds, W. (1996). *Abortion at work: Ideology and practice in a feminist clinic*. Piscataway, NJ: Rutgers University Press.

Simpson, R., Hughes, J., Slutskaya, N., & Balta, M. (2014). Sacrifice and distinction in dirty work: Men's construction of meaning in the butcher trade. *Work, Employment and Society, 28*(5), 754–770.

Staub, E., & Vollhardt, J. (2008). Altruism born of suffering: The roots of caring and helping after victimization and other trauma. *American Journal of Orthopsychiatry, 78*(3), 267–280. https://doi.org/10.1037/a0014223.

Suchman, M. C. (1995). Managing legitimacy: Strategic and institutional approaches. *Academy of Management Review, 20*(3), 571–610.

Suddaby, R., Bitektine, A., & Haack, P. (2017). Legitimacy. *Academy of Management Annals, 11*(1), 451–478.

Sutton, R. I., & Callahan, A. L. (1987). The stigma of bankruptcy: Spoiled organizational image and its management. *Academy of Management Journal, 30*(3), 405–436.

Thomas, V. L., & Fowler, K. (2016). Examining the impact of brand transgressions on consumers' perceptions of celebrity endorsers. *Journal of Advertising*, *45*(4), 377–390. https://doi.org/10.1080/00913367.2016.1172385.

Thomson, S. B., & Grandy, G. (2018). *Stigmas, work and organizations*. New York, NY: Springer.

Tibbals, C. A. (2013). Sex work, office work: Women working behind the scenes in the US adult film industry. *Gender, Work & Organization*, *20*(1), 20–35.

Tilcsik, A., Anteby, M., & Knight, C. R. (2015). Concealable stigma and occupational segregation: Toward a theory of gay and lesbian occupations. *Administrative Science Quarterly*, *60*(3), 446–481.

Timming, A. R., Nickson, D., Re, D., & Perrett, D. (2017). What do you think of my ink? Assessing the effects of body art on employment chances. *Human Resource Management*, *56*(1), 133–149.

Titus Jr., V. K., Parker, O., & Bass, A. E. (2018). Ripping off the band-aid: Scrutiny bundling in the wake of social disapproval. *Academy of Management Journal*, *61*(2), 637–660.

Toubiana, M. (2020). Once in orange always in orange? Identity paralysis and the enduring influence of institutional logics on identity. *Academy of Management Journal*, *63*(6), 1739–1774.

Toubiana, M., & Ruebottom, T. (2022). Stigma hierarchies: The internal dynamics of stigmatization in the sex work occupation. *Administrative Science Quarterly*, *67*(2), 515–552.

Tracey, P., & Phillips, N. (2016). Managing the consequences of organizational stigmatization: Identity work in a social enterprise. *Academy of Management Journal*, *59*(3), 740–765.

Tsai, A. C., Bangsberg, D. R., Kegeles, S. M., et al. (2013). Internalized stigma, social distance, and disclosure of HIV seropositivity in rural Uganda. *Annals of Behavioral Medicine*, *46*(3), 285–294.

Tsui-Auch, L. S., Huang, D., Yang, J. J., & Koh, S. Z. (2022). Double trouble: Containing public disapproval arising from an interplay of stigmatized categories. *Journal of Management Studies*, *59*(8), 2101–2123.

Tyler, I. (2018). Resituating Erving Goffman: From stigma power to black power. *The Sociological Review*, *66*(4), 744–765.

Tyler, I. (2020). *Stigma: The machinery of inequality*. Zed Books: London.

Tyler, I., & Slater, T. (2018). Rethinking the sociology of stigma. *The Sociological Review*, *66*(4), 721–743.

Van Portfliet, M. Resistance Will Be Futile? The Stigmatization (or Not) of Whistleblowers. *J Bus Ethics* **175**, 451–464 (2022). https://doi.org/10.1007/s10551-020-04673-4.

van Vlijmen, J. (2019). Being a cleaner in the Netherlands: Coping with the dirty work stigma. *Facilities*, *37*(5/6), 280–291. https://doi.org/10.1108/F-03-2018-0038.

Vergne, J.-P. (2012). Stigmatized categories and public disapproval of organizations: A mixed-methods study of the global arms industry, 1996–2007. *Academy of Management Journal*, *55*(5), 1027–1052.

Vickers, M. H. (2015). Stories, disability, and "dirty" workers: Creative writing to go beyond too few words. *Journal of Management Inquiry*, *24*(1), 82–89.

Voss, G. (2015). *Stigma and the shaping of the pornography industry*. New York, NY: Routledge.

Walker, S. P. (2008). Accounting, paper shadows and the stigmatised poor. *Accounting, Organizations and Society*, *33*(4–5), 453–487.

Wang, M. S., Raynard, M., & Greenwood, R. (2021a). From grace to violence: Stigmatizing the medical profession in China. *Academy of Management Journal*, *64*(6), 1842–1872.

Wang, M. S., & Tracey, P. (2024). Anti-stigma organizing in the age of social media: How social movement organizations leverage affordances to build solidarity. *Academy of Management Review*, *49*(4), 799–823.

Wang, X., Reger, R. K., & Pfarrer, M. D. (2021b). Faster, hotter, and more linked in: Managing social disapproval in the social media era. *Academy of Management Review*, *46*(2), 275–298.

Washington, M., & Zajac, E. J. (2005). Status evolution and competition: Theory and evidence. *Academy of Management Journal*, *48*(2), 282–296.

Wells-Barnett, I. B., & Royster, J. J. (1997). *Southern Horrors and other writings: The anti-lynching campaign of Ida B. Wells, 1892–1900*. Boston, MA, Bedford Books.

Werner, M. D., Punzi, M. C., & Turkenburg, A. J. K. (2024). Period power: Organizational stigma, multimodality, and social entrepreneurship in the menstrual products industry. *Journal of Management Studies*, *61*(5), 2137–2180.

Wiesenfeld, B. M., Wurthmann, K. A., & Hambrick, D. C. (2008). The stigmatization and devaluation of elites associated with corporate failures: A process model. *The Academy of Management Review*, *33*(1), 231–251.

Wolfe, A. W., & Blithe, S. J. (2015). Managing image in a core-stigmatized organization: Concealment and revelation in Nevada's legal brothels. *Management Communication Quarterly*, *29*(4), 539–563.

Wry, T., Lounsbury, M., & Glynn, M. A. (2011). Legitimating nascent collective identities: Coordinating cultural entrepreneurship. *Organization Science*, *22*(2), 449–463.

Yu, T., Sengul, M., & Lester, R. H. (2008). Misery loves company: The spread of negative impacts resulting from an organizational crisis. *Academy of Management Review*, *33*(2), 452–472.

Yue, L. Q., Rao, H., & Ingram, P. (2013). Information spillovers from protests against corporations: A tale of Walmart and target. *Administrative Science Quarterly*, *58*(4), 669–701.

Zavyalova, A., Bundy, J., & Humphrey, S. E. (2022). A relational theory of reputational stability and change. *Organization Science*, *33*(5), 1724–1740.

Zavyalova, A., Pfarrer, M. D., & Reger, R. K. (2017). Celebrity and infamy? The consequences of media narratives about organizational identity. *Academy of Management Review*, *42*(3), 461–480.

Zavyalova, A., Pfarrer, M. D., Reger, R. K., & Hubbard, T. D. (2016). Reputation as a benefit and a burden? How stakeholders' organizational identification affects the role of reputation following a negative event. *Academy of Management Journal*, *59*(1), 253–276.

Zavyalova, A., Pfarrer, M. D., Reger, R. K., & Shapiro, D. L. (2012). Managing the message: The effects of firm actions and industry spillovers on media coverage following wrongdoing. *Academy of Management Journal*, *55*(5), 1079–1101.

Zhang, R., Wang, M. S., Toubiana, M., & Greenwood, R. (2021). Stigma beyond levels: Advancing research on stigmatization. *Academy of Management Annals*, *15*(1), 188–222.

Cambridge Elements

Organization Theory

Nelson Phillips
UC Santa Barbara

Nelson Phillips is the Abu Dhabi Chamber Professor of Strategy and Innovation at Imperial College London. His research interests include organization theory, technology strategy, innovation, and entrepreneurship, often studied from an institutional theory perspective.

Royston Greenwood
University of Alberta

Royston Greenwood is the Telus Professor of Strategic Management at the University of Alberta, a visiting professor at the University of Cambridge, and a visiting professor at the University of Edinburgh. His research interests include organizational change and professional misconduct.

Advisory Board

Paul Adler *USC*
Mats Alvesson *Lund University*
Steve Barley *University of Santa Barbara*
Jean Bartunek *Boston College*
Paul Hirsch *Northwestern University* Ann Langley *HEC Montreal* Renate Meyer *WU Vienna*
Danny Miller
HEC Montreal
Mike Tushman *Harvard University*
Andrew Van de Ven *University of Minnesota*

About the Series

Organization theory covers many different approaches to understanding organizations. Its focus is on what constitutes the how and why of organizations and organizing, bringing understanding of organizations in a holistic way. The purpose of Elements in Organization Theory is to systematize and contribute to our understanding of organizations.

Cambridge Elements

Organization Theory

Elements in the Series

Cultural Entrepreneurship: A New Agenda for the Study of Entrepreneurial Processes and Possibilities
Michael Lounsbury and Mary Ann Glynn

Emotions in Organization Theory
Charlene Zietsma, Madeline Toubiana, Maxim Voronov and Anna Roberts

Professional Occupations and Organizations
Daniel Muzio, Sundeep Aulakh and Ian Kirkpatrick

Organizational Learning from Performance Feedback: A Behavioral Perspective on Multiple Goals: A Multiple Goals Perspective
Pino G. Audia and Henrich R. Greve

Health Care Research and Organization Theory
Trish Reay, Elizabeth Goodrick and Thomas D'Aunno

The Search for the Virtuous Corporation
Justin O'Brien

Optimal Distinctiveness: A New Agenda for the Study of Competitive Positioning of Organizations and Markets
Eric Yanfei Zhao

Organizational Paradox
Medhanie Gaim, Stewart Clegg, Miguel Pina e Cunha and Marco Berti

Ambiguity in Organization Theory: From Intrinsic to Strategic Perspectives
Giulia Cappellaro, Amelia Compagni and Eero Vaara

Family Firm: A Distinctive Form of Organization
Evelyn Micelotta, Carlotta Benedetti and Paola Rovelli

A Connected World : Social Networks and Organizations
Martin Kilduff, Lei Liu and Stefano Tasselli

Organizational Stigma
Bryant Ashley Hudson, Karen D.W. Patterson and Lin Dong

A full series listing is available at: www.cambridge.org/EORT

For EU product safety concerns, contact us at Calle de José Abascal, 56–1°,
28003 Madrid, Spain or eugpsr@cambridge.org.

www.ingramcontent.com/pod-product-compliance
Lightning Source LLC
LaVergne TN
LVHW011858060526
838200LV00054B/4397